FOLLOWING IN T[HE FOOTSTEP]S
OF

OLIVER CROMWELL

FOLLOWING IN THE FOOTSTEPS OF

OLIVER CROMWELL

A HISTORICAL GUIDE TO THE CIVIL WAR

JAMES HOBSON

PEN & SWORD HISTORY

AN IMPRINT OF PEN & SWORD BOOKS LTD.
YORKSHIRE – PHILADELPHIA

First published in Great Britain in 2019 by
Pen and Sword History
An imprint of
Pen & Sword Books Ltd
Yorkshire - Philadelphia

Copyright © James Hobson, 2019

ISBN 978 1 52673 483 9

The right of James Hobson to be identified as Author of this work has been
asserted by him in accordance with the Copyright, Designs and Patents Act 1988.

A CIP catalogue record for this book is available from the British Library.

Typeset in Ehrhardt MT Std 11.5/14 by
Aura Technology and Software Services, India

Printed and bound in the UK by TJ International Ltd.

Pen & Sword Books Ltd incorporates the Imprints of Pen & Sword Books
Archaeology, Atlas, Aviation, Battleground, Discovery, Family History, History,
Maritime, Military, Naval, Politics, Railways, Select, Transport, True Crime,
Fiction, Frontline Books, Leo Cooper, Praetorian Press, Seaforth Publishing,
Wharncliffe and White Owl.

For a complete list of Pen & Sword titles please contact

PEN & SWORD BOOKS LIMITED
47 Church Street, Barnsley, South Yorkshire, S70 2AS, England
E-mail: enquiries@pen-and-sword.co.uk
Website: www.pen-and-sword.co.uk

or

PEN AND SWORD BOOKS
1950 Lawrence Rd, Havertown, PA 19083, USA
E-mail: Uspen-and-sword@casematepublishers.com
Website: www.penandswordbooks.com

'For my mother, Barbara'

Contents

PART THREE – EVERYBODY

PART FOUR – A BODY

Introduction

In November 1640, a select group of 150 aristocrats and 300 gentlemen met in the Palace of Westminster. There was an atmosphere of crisis. Apart from a short and quarrelsome assembly earlier in the year, this was the first meeting of Parliament for over a decade. This present assembly had been called by Charles I from a position of weakness – he did not have enough money to fund his religious war with Scotland – and the politicians regarded this weakness as their opportunity to put right political and religious injustices that had rankled and accumulated for decades.

One of these Members of Parliament stood out less than most. He was certainly a member of the same ruling class, but he held on to this status by his fingertips. He lived in an eight-roomed cottage and earned his living collecting rent and tithes for the Church of England. Although he had servants crammed into his small house, and directed the work of other men, he had no vast acres of land, no tenants and no history of national political influence. A few years earlier, his life had been even less grand – he was a farmer, renting his land from others.

Not only was he probably the poorest person in the House of Commons on that November day in 1640, there were thousands of people not present who were much more important than him. He was one of the members for Cambridge – an important university town, to be sure, but he was not well known even there. He did not live in Cambridge, but in a nearby backwater, and nobody was quite sure how he had managed to get himself elected.

Theories about his success in Cambridge varied – he had stood up for the poor against the rich, and was connected (ever so distantly) to some rich families in Essex by the good fortune of a marriage connection.

His membership of an earlier parliament, in 1628, was definitely due to the influence of others. There were people with his surname in places of power and responsibility – but if you mentioned his name, it wouldn't ring any bells. He was from a cadet branch of the family, the offspring of a second son, and only by the premature deaths and childlessness of others did he have enough money to call himself a gentleman again.

His best years had passed. He was now a middle-aged man with a reputation for being introspective, intense and moody. He had never been abroad; he had lived in an obscure triangle of Fenland towns linked only by the sluggish river Ouse. He had been routinely educated in a provincial grammar school. Although his knowledge of the Bible was prodigious, he was neither particularly well educated nor quick witted. His speeches were noted for their passion but not always for their style or intelligibility. He did not have the smooth rhetorical skills that were honed by exposure to people at the top of society. He was smooth in no way at all; he was a red-faced country bumpkin. One observer noted:

> His dress was far from attracting respect; he rather engaged
> the attention of the house by a slovenly habit; his clothes were
> ill made, entirely out of fashion … the work of an ordinary
> country tailor and no part of his dress of the best materials.

His only real connection with blood were the drops on his collar after he had shaved badly and not cleaned himself up; he could talk well but had no military successes to justify his strident words. The only thing he had ever raised in a conflict was his voice, and that tended to alienate people.

So, this was Oliver Cromwell; 41 years old with eighteen more still to live. In November 1640 it would have been certain that these declining years would be uneventful.

It then took about eleven years for this man to become one of the most important people in British history. How had this happened? This was an age that believed in the Great Chain Of Being, in which each person was allocated a fixed place, with rights and obligations but no real prospect of social mobility. Yet Oliver Cromwell, born a middle-ranking nobody in a declining county family in an obscure part of the country, became the only non-royal ruler of Britain. He organised the only public trial and execution of a king, brutalised parts of the British Isles in an attempt to unite them, changed religious and political life forever, and still divides people today.

This book is not a biography of Cromwell, nor a detailed description of his battles. Professor John Morrill, who first introduced me to Cromwell at Cambridge University in the late 1970s, estimated that there have been 160 full length biographies of Cromwell produced since 1658. He doesn't need another one, at least not from me!

Instead, this book follows his footsteps – physically and mentally. No assumption is made that the places will all be visited, scattered as they are over the UK and Ireland; but the book will add to any visit, either in person or as an inspiration to find out more. There will also be an attempt to work out what was happening in Cromwell's mind as he passed through these physical and political landscapes, while always being aware of the danger of overreach. The second part of the book considers his reputation after death, when everybody constructed a Cromwell that suited them – something that continues to this day, and is conclusive proof that he still matters.

Part One

NOBODY

Chapter One

The Cromwell Family
1559–1610
Hinchingbrooke House, Huntingdon

Oliver Cromwell was born on 25 April 1599 to a comfortable, landowning family in Huntingdon in the East of England. He and his kin were members of the gentry; they owned property, lived by the rents and labour of others, and were entitled and obliged to take part in the affairs of the local community. In future years, both his friends and enemies had reason to exaggerate the lowliness of his birth. The truth is that young Oliver's life seemed destined to be, in the words of his biographer Antonia Fraser, 'unremarkable but not unpleasant'.

The extended Cromwell family were much nearer the top than the bottom of seventeenth-century society. Above his family were an aristocratic landed elite with wealth and power, and below them the 'middling sort' of skilled workers, underpinned by a mass of agricultural workers who had no property except their labour, no economic security and no voice in society.

Cromwell was not born into an easy life, but it was more comfortable than most. In an age of merciless infant mortality and the real likelihood of crippling, deforming and life-limiting diseases, the Cromwells were one of thousands that could at least rule out the likelihood of being poor and powerless. Given a fair amount of luck, Cromwell would become one of the thousands of gentlemen in this middle rank of society with middling contributions to local government. Nothing was guaranteed, however; individual fortunes within the family could fall as well as rise; not all members of the extended family were equally endowed with wealth, and Oliver's direct family were the poor relations. In 1654 he made the observation to his first Parliament that he 'was by birth a gentleman living neither in any considerable height, nor in obscurity'; although this accurately shows his social status, too much attention is given to the word 'gentleman' and not enough to the fact that he was 'born' there. Social status, like life, was precarious.

For those who get confused by the two great Cromwells of history, Thomas and Oliver, it may be reassuring to know that Henry VIII's famous, infamous and ruthless advisor was a relation of Oliver's – admittedly in a less than straightforward way. Thomas Cromwell had an elder sister, Katharine, and in 1494 she married a London-based Welshman called Morgan Williams. This was decades before Thomas Cromwell became famous – he was only 10 at the time of this lowly marriage of social equals – the daughter of a Putney butcher to the local brewer. The skill of the Williams family was to exploit their good fortune, supporting the religious changes of Henry VIII, and in the 1530s the family changed their name to Cromwell, with the king's permission. Both Morgan and his son, the first Cromwell (Richard born c. 1502, died 1544) were enthusiastic enablers of Henry VIII's plan to dissolve the monasteries and they benefited, like others, by receiving former church property at knock-down prices.

It may seem clever to change your name to that of one of the king's most influential ministers, but it was more complicated than this at the time. For a start, the name was not changed again when Thomas Cromwell fell from power. This was partly because Henry soon recanted his hasty decision to execute Thomas, but mostly because other Welsh families abandoned their names at the same time. Henry thought it better to have family surnames rather than use the patronymic Welsh system. Welsh surnames became politically inconvenient if families wished to prosper, so all Welsh names were anglicised. For many, the change was easy – 'ap Richard' became Pritchard, 'ap Robert' became Probert and 'ap Harry' was transformed to Parry. 'Morgan ap Williams' would normally become just Williams, but this would not have been a recognisable surname in England at the time. So the ambitious family were pleased to accept their new prestigious English surname.

So Oliver Cromwell, a descendant of this marriage, was really Oliver Williams, and the man called 'God's Englishman' by his fervent supporters, was originally Welsh. After Cromwell's death, many branches of the family reverted to their original name, when the social stigma of being Welsh was overshadowed by the disgrace of being a Cromwell. Even before the rise and fall of Oliver, members of the family called themselves 'Cromwell alias Williams' on legal documents.

Hinchingbrooke House near Huntingdon was the Cromwell family's main prize for supporting the assault on the Catholic Church. Oliver visited and played in this house as a small child. It would have been a mostly Tudor mansion, but the ruins of the catholic nunnery would still have been visible. It would have been a daily reminder that the end of Catholicism in England was the beginning of the family's prosperity, and that there was nothing more important than the patronage of the monarch.

Hinchingbrooke still has Tudor original features – the remains of a Great Chamber, Tudor beams and plasterwork. There is part of a surviving wall-painting showing Sir Richard Cromwell at a jousting match with Henry VIII. Oliver Cromwell, playing in the house, would have looked up and seen the Tudor rose carved into the ceiling and may have been told about the visit of Queen Elizabeth in 1564. Oliver Cromwell, Robert's elder brother was knighted by Queen Elizabeth in 1598. Oliver would have been under no doubt where the family's loyalties lay. The Cromwells, like all successful gentry families, were monarchists.

Loyalty to the monarch is displayed on the outside of the building as well. The most famous outside feature, dated 1602, just as the Tudor dynasty was about to end, shows both the monarch's and Cromwell's coats of arms.

The Cromwells also enjoyed a strong relationship with the new Stuart monarchy, and the main reason for that was geographical. Hinchingbrooke was near enough to the Great North Road to be convenient for the new James I. Any journey from Edinburgh to London would pass through Huntingdon, and in April 1603, the new king travelled there as he processed from his old to his new court

The future Charles I would also have visited the house as a child and young Oliver would have been aware of the many visits of James I, mostly in November each year for the hawking. The family were also painfully aware of how much money Sir Oliver was spending on hospitality for the king. There is written evidence of James writing to him telling him not to shoot the estate's game birds until the king arrived to shoot them himself.

A contemporary history, Stowe's *Annals* reports the importance and expense of these royal visits:

> There attended at Master Oliver Cromwell's house, he says,
> the Head of the University of Cambridge, all clad in scarlet

gowns and corner caps, who having presence of his Majesty, there was made a learned and eloquent oration in Latin, welcoming his Majesty, as also entreating the confirmation of their privileges, which his highness most willingly granted.

Master Cromwell presented his Majesty with many rich and valuable presents, as a very great and faire-wrought standing cup of gold, goodly horses, deep mouthed hounds, ... hawks of excellent wing, and at the remove gave fifty pounds amongst his Majesty's officers.

James visited again in March 1617 for another state visit, when the king was making his way reluctantly *to* Scotland this time. With him was his chaplain Dr Laud, later to be arrested, imprisoned and executed by the Puritan Parliament for his alleged Catholic sympathies, with Cromwell at the forefront.

As welcome as they were, Oliver and his father Robert would always be visitors and – literally and metaphorically – poor relations. Despite this, Robert Cromwell's family were only one (largish) step from monarchy itself. The Royalist hack writer James Heath suggested that young Oliver had given his future king a black eye at Hinchingbrooke. It suited the Royalists to suggest that Cromwell's hatred of his rightful king was bred in the bone of a devilish child. One of the reasons that it had some credibility is that both youngsters inhabited the same sphere – but only just.

The Cromwell family's link with the crown has been used as evidence by some historians that they were an important family, but their dealings with the monarchy dragged them down. Although Sir Oliver gained socially from the association, it was never a sound financial investment. While other members of the gentry invested in agricultural improvement, the Cromwell family invested in the Stuart monarchy, an organisation which never paid its debts with money. Sir Oliver regularly sold off his other assets and he offered to sell Hinchingbrooke in 1624 to King James, hoping to lease it back on favourable terms. James died the next year and the sale did not happen; in any case, the Stuarts were fonder of forcing loans out of the gentry than offering them.

The house was sold to Sir Sidney Montague in June 1627 and their family history is part of any visit to Hinchingbrooke, which is open to the public. The £6,000 price tag cleared Sir Oliver's debt, for a short time anyway. Sir Oliver was destined to live for another thirty years in fenland obscurity and supported his king when the civil war started, endangering his fortune for a second time. His remaining property was at Ramsey Abbey, Cambridgeshire, another house built by an earlier Cromwell over the ruins of a pre-Reformation abbey. The sale of Hinchingbrooke was a setback for the whole Cromwell family, and by the late 1620s it seemed clear that this particular gentry family were fading quite fast.

Family loyalty still mattered, even when war came. In May 1643, Cromwell visited his uncle with a troop of soldiers and removed weapons and silver plate to fund Parliament's war effort. In April 1648, Sir Oliver was given some of his property back through the influence of the now more famous Oliver, who visited his uncle un-hatted, showing his respect to a more senior member of the family in the traditional way.

Charles I and his Catholic wife, Henrietta Maria, spent two days at Hinchingbrooke in 1635 as guests of the new owners. Charles spent another night there as a prisoner of a Parliamentary Army in 1647 on his way to have his future decided by Cromwell. The occupier from 1644 was Edward Montague, who fought on Parliament's side in the war. Montague was present when the decision was made to raise an army in Eastern England to fight against the king – and the leading light in that organisation was Cromwell, who was eager to create a more disciplined fighting force. Despite being only 18, Edward Montague raised his own regiment, and eventually became a major general and confidante of Cromwell. As General at Sea, his quick action smoothed the way to the accession of Richard Cromwell in 1658. Like many others, he seamlessly changed sides, escorted Charles II back to England in 1660 and died in the king's service at the sea battle at Sole Bay in 1672.

Chapter Two

Formative Years
1610–1617
High Street, Huntingdon
St John's Grammar School, Huntingdon
Sidney Sussex College, Cambridge

Oliver's father Robert was a second-born son, who could never prosper like a first-born due to the English tradition of primogeniture. When Robert Cromwell's father died in 1604, Robert was bequeathed a modest town house in Huntingdon while the eldest son, Sir Oliver, took control of Hinchingbrooke and other substantial properties.

Cromwell's birthplace was demolished and rebuilt in the 1830s and is now used as a care home. The care home website does mention the fact quite prominently, and the facade has a Cromwell coat of arms and a plaque. However, it is not really the actual home of Cromwell; there are only a few bricks and features left from the original thirteenth-century building. The website also advertises the highly convenient location in the middle of the town, and this was also the case in the seventeenth century; it has a prominent location at 82 High Street. Later in his life, Cromwell moved to inaccessible parts of the Fens, but he was not born in the middle of nowhere. He was literally born on the road to London.

Just like Hinchingbrooke House, 82 High Street came into the family as part of the proceeds of the dissolution of the monasteries. The house belonged to the Austen Friars until the 1540s and it passed to the Cromwells as a reward for their loyalty to Henry VIII. The land and buildings were purchased by Sir Henry Cromwell for his son Robert, who demolished the ruined friary and built a new house. Robert lived there for nearly half a century; it passed to his son Oliver in 1617 who in turn sold it in 1631 when he moved to St Ives. Robert's wife Elizabeth (Oliver's mother) continued to live there as a tenant in what must have been straitened circumstances.

Oliver's father would have been the first big influence in his life. The information we have about Robert Cromwell is not very specific. His income suggested the lower strata of the gentry; he played his part in the local administration of the town. Robert was briefly an MP in 1593 and was a Justice of the Peace and a Town Councillor. His income allowed him to be seen as a gentlemen – just about, but it was the family name that gave him most of his social standing.

At the age of 11, after having a private tutor – a Mr Long – since the age of 7, Oliver was sent to the free school attached to the hospital of St John in Huntingdon, a few minutes' walk to the other end of the High Street, run in Cromwell's time by Dr Thomas Beard. The fact that he went to school rather than being educated at home shows that the family was nowhere near the top of English society.

He spent six years at this school, and Dr Thomas Beard was the first non-family influence on Cromwell's life. Beard was a friend of the family, so we can assume that the young Oliver received the type of education that the family wanted. The family would not have handed their son over to Beard randomly or by accident. The start of formal education was the end of childhood at this time, and the beginning of moulding the man. Beard was meant to be an influence on their son. We worry today that schools are used by religious bigots to teach extreme versions of established faiths, but that is exactly what would have happened in Cromwell's school in Huntingdon; and it would have been done with the express approval of Cromwell's parents. Similar families all over the country would be doing the same.

Beard's influence would have been all-pervasive. He was Oliver's teacher on weekdays and his preacher on Sundays. The ethos was religious and academic and the punishment was corporal. We know that Cromwell took part in didactic plays and Beard had the personal responsibility of tutoring him for Cambridge University. However, we have almost no specific information about what Cromwell did at school from sources we can trust – we can only generalise from what we know about the teacher and the ethos of the school. We do not even know if Cromwell was a good student, although later in life he was able to converse with the Dutch ambassador in Latin.

What was Cromwell taught in this modest, single-room school? Beard was already famous for his 1597 book *The Theatre of God's Judgement* – his message being that God punishes sin in this life, not just post-mortem, and it was vital to the health of the soul to seek God's signs on earth. Beard was one of the sources for the grisly death of Christopher Marlowe, a playwright accused of other sins that would have made a Puritan enraged; but the 'playwright' part was enough of an accusation.

From our point of view, Cromwell's education was biased and partisan. Beard would have transmitted an unrelenting hatred and fear of Roman Catholics. Anti-Catholicism was very much a live issue when Cromwell was at school. Dr Beard had arrived at St John's in 1604, the year before the Gunpowder plot, when Cromwell was 5 years old. The Pope was the antichrist and Catholicism was an ever-present threat to the continued existence of England. This was not a novel idea in early Stuart England; it was the vehemence that was different. There would be no shortage of lurid stories of traitors and terrorists; the Spanish Armada of 1588 was still within living memory, and Cromwell would have been taught that it was God that scattered the Spanish fleet with His rather unfortunately entitled 'Protestant Wind'.

The next three teachings were linked: predestination, the elect and the need for a godly reformation of morality and manners. God knew all and was timeless, therefore He knew who was already saved from damnation – they had already been chosen at the beginning of creation. So the elect already existed, and an individual's good work and charity in the future could not change this. Your personal salvation and that of others depended on a reformation of manners and an improvement in moral behaviour, which, while vital for the community, could not guarantee a salvation that had already been decided.

So, in an already religious age, Cromwell received a supercharged religious education. Was Cromwell paying attention? Was he a Puritan when he left school? Until recently, most historians would have said yes to both questions, but the actual evidence is rather scant. Historian John Morrill has even speculated that Beard was not always a convincing Puritan. He never actually tried to move outside the Church of England and was very interested in collecting more paid jobs – he was 'a greedy pluralist'.

The Grammar School in Huntingdon was originally the great hall of the Hospital of St John the Baptist – think 'hospitality' rather than 'hospital'. It survived the ransacking of the church in the sixteenth century and was converted into a school in 1565. The building was ancient even before Cromwell was there; the front has Norman arches with the traditional dog-tooth decoration around the outside. It is uncertain how much of the building Cromwell would recognise today because the facade was heavily 'medievalised' by an unfortunate Victorian improvement campaign in the 1870s. By a coincidence, the former Grammar School is now located on the premises of Hinchingbrooke House.

The museum, like the Tudor schoolroom it replaced, is one room, although in Cromwell's time there would have been an upper floor for the school master. Apart from the chance to be in the exact spot where Cromwell's early world-view may have been created, the museum has a variety of artefacts, many of them lent by Cromwell's relatives (his direct family became extinct in the 1820s). This includes a range of portraits of Cromwell, his family and his contemporaries. One of the problems with evidence of the civil war is the lack of contemporary painting of the actual battles – it was a common art form on the Continent but not in England. The museum has some examples of Victorian civil war battlefields which always portray them as much less grisly than they really were.

There are also some articles that are strongly believed to be Cromwell's personal possessions – there is a powder flask with 'OC' on it, adorned with amber, ivory and mother of pearl – not really very puritan. A seventeenth-century wide-brimmed hat and a sword, both associated with Cromwell, are on display. Being made out of felt rather than metal, the hat is a remarkable survivor of the civil war. Like all museums with even the slightest connection with the conflict, there is a full-size replica pike to remind you of the pure physical effort of warfare.

The museum has one of Britain's best collections of Cromwelliana – indeed it is the only UK museum entirely devoted to Oliver and his family. Some items are modest, relating to his period of obscurity in the Fens, but some are very grand, as befits a man who ruled Britain between 1653 and 1658. Cromwell's escutcheon – an emblem bearing a coat of arms used to drape his coffin, can be seen there, as can one of the plaster copies of his death mask (the original wax version can be seen at the British Museum, with other plaster copies at the Ashmolean in Oxford and Bolling Hall Museum, Bradford)

Cromwell received expensive gifts as Lord Protector. He liked to be given hawks and horses, as befitted a country gentlemen, but the museum has some excellent artefacts that have survived. There is an impressive perfume cabinet, a gift from the Grand Duke of Tuscany, and a medicine chest of the highest quality by the Bavarian silversmith Kolb of Augsburg. This still contains seventeenth-century tools and instruments. Cromwell suffered throughout his life with the tertian ague (malaria) and, some would argue, a bit of hypochondria as well.

Opposite the museum is the church of All Saints. The exterior has not changed much since Cromwell's time, apart from the red-brick tower built to replace the one destroyed by Royalist cannon in 1645. Oliver's father and many children of Sir Oliver Cromwell are buried there, marked by a plaque in front of the pulpit which shows its approximate location. It is probable that the family monuments were destroyed by the Royalists – a harsh judgement on the 'loyal' members of the family who were not implicated in Cromwell's actions, and similar to the attitude of the vengeful Royalists to the bodies of Cromwell's wife and relations after the restoration.

The vault itself was sealed up in the twentieth century. This is where Cromwell would have been buried had he not become the most powerful non-royal person in British history. The font over which Cromwell and eight of his children were baptised can also be seen at All Saints, although Cromwell was baptised on 29 April 1599 at the now demolished church of St John, with the font later moved to All Saints. All Saints has the parish register of births; Cromwell's baptism is written in Latin while the ones around it are in English; it seems that this change was made later. A critic and vandal had added 'England's plague for five years' which was later scored out. The names below Cromwell are partly obscured by the generations of fingers and sleeves touching the document.

On Market Hill, in sight of the museum and church, is the Falcon Inn. Records suggest that Cromwell used the inn as a base to recruit puritan-inclined soldiers in 1643. It is an old coaching house, over 100 years old when Cromwell was there. When Cromwell was 13, in October 1612, the body of Mary Queen of Scots passed through the High Street, passing his school. It spent the night at All Hallows on the way from Peterborough to a new, grand tomb at Westminster Abbey on the orders of James I. James's mother had been horribly executed in 1587; his son was to suffer the same fate, and in 1612 the person mostly responsible for it was a young man on the same street, and he too would be buried in Westminster Abbey.

On 23 April 1616, coincidentally the date of Shakespeare's death, Cromwell was admitted to Sydney Sussex College Cambridge. Cromwell had not moved far either geographically or spiritually from his family. Oliver did not follow his father and uncle, who both attended Queen's College; the family made the deliberate choice to send him to a very puritan college run by Dr Samuel Ward – a man with a strong belief in predestination. With Doctor Ward and his personal tutor Dr Howlett, this arrangement seemed to be more schooling of the Thomas Beard type.

It is difficult to establish the influence of Sidney Sussex on Cromwell. He was there for less than a year and never graduated, as his father died in 1617. Cromwell was a privileged student – he was a fellow commoner, living in extra luxury and paying above the already high fee level to do so. This extra fee would have exempted him from acting as a servant to his fellow students, but would have cost between £30 and £50 a year – so it would have been a decision financed and planned by the wider family.

Some of the sources from the period of school and university seem to show a boisterous, easy going young man whose activities verged on the naughty – by our standards a 'normal teenager'. Most of these are written by hostile biographers, but it does seem strange that they did not impute a fanatical puritanism that would have served them better in damaging his reputation than comments about drinking and football. Instead, his enemies recounted stories of him roistering, performing plays and generally being a typical gentlemen; but in truth we don't know.

Cromwell has had a variable relationship with his alma mater since then, but in 1960 there was reconciliation when Cromwell's embalmed head, the only piece of him that survived the post mortem execution in 1661, was secretly buried in the college, with a plaque that seems simultaneously understated and boastful.

Near to
this place was buried
on March 25 1960 the head of
OLIVER CROMWELL
Lord Protector of the Common
Wealth of England, Scotland &
Ireland, Fellow Commoner
of this college 1616–1617

The chapel in Cromwell's time would have been a reassuringly puritan building, financed by the strictly protestant Countess of Sussex, whose will instructed that the new college be called 'Lady Frances Sidney Sussex College' after herself. The place where Cromwell lies is mostly an eighteenth-century ornate baroque creation that Cromwell would not have liked very much.

It is said that only three people know the exact location of the head at the present time. I was a student at the university in the late 1970s and some reactionary (and, to be fair, usually inebriated) students were looking for him. His ghost has been spotted there, inevitably. Ghosts of Cromwell seem to be particularly active in places where there are tourists – a remarkable but quite common psychic phenomenon.

Despite Cromwell's connection with Cambridge, there has been little recognition of him there. He was the Member of Parliament for the town from 1640 to 1653 but it was not a place where he actually lived. Around the corner from his college, about two minutes away by foot, is the only public plaque to Cromwell in the city, in the Market Passage at the original site of the Black Bear Inn. Cromwell held meetings there to plan the parliamentary war effort. The plaque itself is moderately controversial, using the words 'Lord Protector of the British Republic'. It was unveiled by the former Conservative prime minister, Sir John Major, in December 2016. Although clearly no Cromwellian, Sir John appreciated the man's importance in his unveiling speech:

> If you look down the long avenue of our history over the last thousand years, there are very few people who have had the same significance on the way Britain lives as Cromwell.

Both Cromwell's friends and enemies could agree with that, especially as Sir John failed to say whether those consequences were for good or for evil.

Chapter Three

Law, Family, Disgrace
London
Huntingdon 1617–1631
St Giles Church, Cripplegate

Cromwell left Cambridge quickly after the death of his father, but it was a rush rather than a panic. In the past, panic was assumed; a young man who was called back to the family home on the death of his father would be indispensable for the rest of the family, which now consisted of a widow and six equally 'helpless' females.

However, Cromwell's return was due to legal issues, not the inability of seventeenth-century women to cope with an emergency. He was still under legal age of responsibility (which was 21) when his father died and there was a danger that he (and his family's property) would become subject to control by the monarch as a 'ward of court'. This did not happen, and Cromwell was on the move again in the same year as his father died. Cromwell was living in London in 1617/18.

It would have been possible to make regular trips from Huntingdon to London but it probably was not necessary. His mother, aided by her family connections, was more than able to cope. Her husband could have chosen anybody to execute his will, and the fact that he chose his wife alone gives strong clues to her competency.

What did he do in London? It would have to have been something useful, and logic suggests that it would have been legal study. It is widely believed that Cromwell attended the Inns of Court, possibly at Lincoln's Inn or perhaps Grey's. His father, his uncle Sir Oliver and his grandfather Sir Henry, had all done the same thing, as had most of Cromwell's contemporaries of similar social standing. Cromwell was to send his own son Richard there in 1647.

It would make sense, even though it cannot be proved. There is no evidence of Cromwell having done so. It was part of the traditional life journey for a member of the middling gentry – school, university, then a smattering of law to enable him to do his local duties as a Justice of the Peace and to understand enough law to buy and sell property. It was not a tragedy for his personal development that he left Cambridge after one year. Failing to graduate would make little difference to his prospects; family connections were much more important.

Although he was in London, his life at Lincoln's Inns Fields would have been semi-rural – the clue being in the name. The area was not to have much development until the 1630s. At this point, with no paperwork associated with life's landmarks, we lose track of him.

In 1620 Cromwell took the next conventional step and was married, on 22 August, to Elizabeth Bourchier, eldest daughter of Sir James Bourchier of Felsted, Essex. The Bourchiers had a townhouse in London and Oliver and Elizabeth were married in the nearest parish church of St Giles Without, Cripplegate. The church still stands today, surrounded by the brutal concrete of the new Barbican. The church survived the Great Fire of London in 1666, but was greatly damaged by the Luftwaffe in 1940. The unusually exact restoration was to a plan of 1545, so Oliver would have recognised most of the outside and much of the layout of the surviving building today. There is a bust to Cromwell in the church and plaques commemorating his marriage there, although you would learn nothing about Elizabeth from the details; her name is not mentioned.

You can tell a lot about the seventeenth-century gentry from the manner of their marriage – most importantly, the way the family were moving socially. Elizabeth's father was a leather and fur seller; but he was no small scale artisan. He was a major London and Essex landowner and businessman who later gave Cromwell some good social contacts. However, it was not an ancient family; James Bourchier was knighted by James I early in 1610 and the coat of arms were of recent origin. There was a member of a more ancient family who signed the death warrant of Charles I – Sir John Bourchier – but he seems to be unrelated to the mercantile newcomers that Oliver's minor gentry family hitched themselves to.

So, in terms of social climbing, the marriage was a score draw, with the Bourchiers having more money and the Cromwells more pedigree. The marriage also casts some doubt on the stories of bad behaviour and lewdness in Cromwell's character – what Noble, a later hostile biographer calls 'the juice of the grape and the charms of the fair'. Cromwell's marriage to this respectable family happened a mere four months after his age of majority, it could not have been much earlier; those who believe the Royalist propaganda that he had wasted both his money and reputation at this early stage need to explain why he was still able to marry well.

Elizabeth Cromwell has not been treated well by history. Royalists called her 'Joan', a name that connoted commonness and vulgarity, and regarded her rise as even more unnatural than Oliver's. She has been portrayed as dull and pedestrian, unable to break out of her limited role as helpmate to a man, even when that man ruled Britain. They loved each other though; Cromwell, not a man to elaborate on such feelings, sent Elizabeth a slightly stuffy letter from Scotland in 1650 saying 'Thou art dearer to me than any creature, let that suffice', and later Elizabeth replied that, 'my life is but half a life in your absence', although she did not spell it as accurately as that.

We do not know how they met. It may have been in East Anglia, where Cromwell had family, or it may have been in London, where the Bourchiers would often reside. Elizabeth was born and baptised in 1598 in Felsted, Essex, but the rest of James's children were baptised in All Hallows Barking, another church that is just about recognisable today after the depredations of fire, the Victorians and the Luftwaffe.

When Cromwell ruled, this church where his wife and sisters-in-law were baptised was given a stocks and whipping post. Some statues were later defaced by Puritans. It was also damaged in a massive explosion nearby in April 1649, and probably coincidentally, was one of the few church restorations during Cromwell's rule as Lord Protector.

There is a lot to see at St Giles Cripplegate for those interested in the period. Shakespeare would have attended services here, and John Milton, poet, writer and Cromwell's Latin Secretary (or propagandist), died in 1674 and is buried here. Another propagandist who would have influenced Cromwell even more is also commemorated here – John Foxe, the author of the 'Book of Martyrs', a compendium of Protestants murdered for their faith, described in graphic detail.

The church is open to visitors when not performing its function as a parish church – when you stand outside you can see the modern Cromwell Tower looming high, part of the complex of quickly built but prestigious homes surrounded by buildings dedicated to trade and profit. Apart from the use of concrete rather than brick, it could be argued that not that much has changed fundamentally in the 400 years since Cromwell married there.

Cromwell moved away from London after his marriage, returning to Huntingdon – he may have moved back from the capital even before his marriage. Children appeared quickly and at regular intervals, with the family's share of infant and baby deaths. The couple had nine children in total, with only five outliving them. In the 264 months between her marriage and the birth of their last child Frances in 1638, Elizabeth was pregnant for at least eighty-one of them, not including possible miscarriages of which we are unaware. This fact, while not being exceptional – Elizabeth's mother had twelve children – shows the strength of Stuart women.

Having done all the things a member of the gentry needed to do, his life now seemed to be set – to be lived conscientiously, with some minor provincial achievements, and then forgotten after two generations. The Historian Thomas Carlyle, a fan of Cromwell's, describes the life people like Cromwell could expect:

> he might here have continued unnoticeable … farming lands, most probably attending quarter sessions, doing the civic … and social duties in the common way, living as his father before him had done.

That is – initially – what happened. Huntingdon was an administrative centre for the county of Cambridgeshire, and the records suggest that Cromwell played his part. The website *www.historyofparliamentonline.org* suggests that he was member of the Common Council for most of the 1620s, briefly a bailiff and a Justice of the Peace for the second half of the decade. He was the junior of two Members of Parliament that the borough of Huntingdon sent to the 1628 Parliament. It was this assembly that saw the first stirrings of discontent against the methods of Charles I. Cromwell seemed to have played little part in proceedings, although they still seemed to have agitated him.

The other, more senior, member selected for the 1628 Parliament was James, of the now dominant Montague family. When Sir Oliver sold Hinchingbrooke in 1627, the Cromwells ceased to be the most prominent family in Huntingdon. The new owners wished to dominate the area in the way the Cromwells had done. He left Huntingdon in 1631. By the time he returned, some thirteen years later, the power balance between Cromwell and the local worthies of the town would be transformed.

Chapter Four

Downwards
St Ives 1631–1636

Cromwell and his family took a step back in 1631 when he ceased to be a major property owner, sold the leasehold of his house in Huntingdon and rented land from his friend Henry Lawrence, 5 miles away in St Ives, Cambridgeshire. The harvests of 1630 and 1631 were terrible. This was a particularly bad time to voluntarily become dependent on what you could grow. Cromwell must have been desperate.

Cromwell's time in Huntingdon ended in humiliation, excluded from the Common Council in 1630 and brought up before the king's Privy Council for insulting the new mayor and accusing him of fraud. He was held briefly in custody in Westminster and was obliged to make a public apology to the mayor. In 1627 his power base disappeared as his family were supplanted and three years later his reputation was gone. The historian Martyn Bennet puts Cromwell's situation in a nutshell, 'a public apology of this kind ... was a personal and political humiliation. Oliver was a disgrace in his own town'. It was time to leave Huntingdon.

This was a step backwards geographically as well as socially – St Ives being an out-of-the-way place that was not even the major town in the county. He was not a popular figure in his home town, but by moving a few miles away to a new jurisdiction he was able to keep away from his enemies while maintaining an interest in local events. He had left Huntingdon under a cloud, with a reputation for attacking the local government oligarchy – some cynics might add that his attacks on the council only started when he was excluded from it by a new town charter in the late 1620s. This clouding of his reputation, and the sale of his grandfather's house at Hinchingbrooke, meant that the Cromwell family would not have the influence to produce an MP for Huntingdon ever again.

The transfer from Huntingdon to St Ives was more of a social descent than a new place to live. Essentially, he sold all of his property (and some of his mother's) and with the proceeds of £1,800, bought sheep and rented land from friends and family. Children born in St Ives continued to be baptised in Huntingdon, including their son James who was born and died in 1632 – baptised on the 7 January and died the next day. This could not have helped the situation; contrary to the current myth, parents did not become inured to the early death of their children. While at St Ives there were no more children born for five years; after they moved to Ely there were two more: Mary (born 1637) and Frances (1638). The reason for lack of fertility in St Ives is unclear; there may have been miscarriages, but it is still quite a long time.

Cromwell was an unhappy Protestant when he lived in St Ives. Some Historians have suggested that when he turned all his assets into cash in 1631 and then just rented houses and bought animals that could easily be sold, he was preparing for emigration to the New World to escape Charles I's version of Protestantism. This was not necessarily part of a personal crisis. It had become a normal thing to do, and emigration was never far from Cromwell's mind until the 1640s. In the 1630s an estimated 17,000 Puritans made the hazardous journey across the Atlantic to escape the religious policies of Charles and Laud. Henry Lawrence, his friend and landlord in St Ives, was directly connected to the Saybrook Company that organised emigration to New England.

There is not much to see that comes from Oliver's time in St Ives. Thomas Carlyle visited the area in 1842 as part of his tour of 'Cromwelldom'. It was a small, dingy town then; Carlyle estimated that in Cromwell's time it would have been no more than a row of houses fronting the river. He felt he could locate Cromwell's farm – 'gross boggy lands fringed with willow trees'. This was, according to Carlyle, the lowest point of the man, and it is not necessary to subscribe to his 'great man theory of history' to agree with him. In his later years, Cromwell was able to look back at this period of his life with good feeling, although it was the type of nostalgia created by battling with argumentative politicians.

> I would have been glad to have lived under my wood side, to have kept a flock of sheep, rather than have undertaken this government. (1658)

19

Cromwell was trying to be wistful and bucolic by mentioning sheep. Perhaps the MPs would have reacted differently if Cromwell had mentioned that he also looked after chickens as well.

Cromwell was thought to have leased Green End Farm and one of that name existed on the outskirts of St Ives at that time – which further helps to put into perspective the size of St Ives. Cromwell probably lived in Slepe Hall as a tenant of Henry Lawrence. (Twenty years later Lawrence was the President of Cromwell's Protectoral Council). It would have been a very large building and it is possible that the Cromwell family would have shared the house with others. The hall was demolished in 1848 and only Cromwell Terrace and Cromwell Place survive as a reminder. The fact that the locals were ready to name roads after Cromwell in the 1850s shows a readiness to acknowledge him and the slightly more favourable Victorian attitude to Cromwell at the time.

The four Cromwell boys – Robert, Richard, Henry and Oliver, were educated at the prestigious Felsted School in Essex – no cramped provincial grammar school for them. The Felsted School was very highly regarded and parents from all over the country used it to educate their children. The headmaster, Martin Holbeach, was highly esteemed as a Puritan teacher. However, Holbeach also had a reputation for successfully copying the classical curriculum of more famous schools such as St Pauls and Westminster. In terms of schooling, the Cromwells were punching way above their weight.

How did they manage it? The marriage broadened the horizons of the Cromwell family and made them new connections; it was a poor seventeenth-century gentry marriage that did not manage to do that. The Bourchiers were the most powerful local family in the area and this, in turn, gave the Cromwells an important connection to the Rich family. The first Rich was an enforcer for Thomas Cromwell in the time of Henry VIII, shown fictionally but accurately in the novels of Hilary Mantel's *Wolf Hall* and Robert Bolt's *A Man for All Seasons*. Richard Rich also founded Felsted School, and his later descendants were part of Cromwell's circle – or more accurately, he was part of theirs. It was family and connections that were exploited ruthlessly in a way that would be perfectly acceptable in the seventeenth century.

Martin Holbeach was also part of Cromwell's circle of Calvinist intellectuals who were dissatisfied with both the religious compromises under Elizabeth and the direction of the church under Charles. Cromwell may have met, or heard about, Holbeach for the first time when they were both Cambridge students – Holbeach was at the other hotbed of Puritanism, Queens College, although he did not matriculate (start his studies) until 1617, the year that Cromwell had to return home. After the Restoration, Holbeach still had a reputation for dissent – it was said that 'he scarcely bred a man that was loyal to his Prince'. Cromwell would have known of this reputation when he entrusted him with his four boys.

Cromwell was not just interested in theology. He was clearly trying to provide a wider education for his sons than he had been given. He gave this advice to his eldest son Richard:

> Read a little history ... study the mathematics and cosmography. These are good with subordination to the things of God. These are fit for public service for which a man is born.

In the end, he was disappointed in his son, who preferred hunting to learning

Oliver took a modest part in the administrative life of St Ives. In both 1633 and 1635, Carlyle noted that his name was on a list of respectable taxpayers given minor responsibilities for Highways and Greens. One of the documents had been defaced and Cromwell's name cut out, and this kind of censorship happened frequently. We will never be fully sure of Cromwell's contribution to local government in St Ives, or anywhere, as defacing documents that mention him was a regular occurrence. This does not disguise the fact that he was a nobody.

Chapter Five

Step Forward?
Ely 1636–1640

In 1636, Oliver Cromwell and his family were saved from impending insignificance by a bequest in a will. Cromwell's uncle on his mother's side, Sir Thomas Stewart, owned property and a tithe farming business in Ely which the family had acquired through their loyalty to Henry VIII when he dissolved the local monasteries in the 1530s. It would transform Oliver's life.

On 30 September 1635, while Cromwell was working for a living in St Ives, Sir Thomas was declared not to be insane. It has been suggested that Cromwell himself had some part in this process, to secure an inheritance for himself and his family. If Thomas was insane, Cromwell would be in control of his estate. There is some circumstantial evidence that links Cromwell to this event; Sir Thomas was noticeably cooler to Cromwell in the last year of his life (1636) and Cromwell's eventual inheritance seemed to have been made deliberately complicated by Sir Thomas.

Some historians believe that Cromwell's ability to tend animals in St Ives without complaint was because he thought his inheritance was guaranteed. This doesn't seem to be the case if he was involved in this legal case. It is possible to be even more uncharitable – he knew it was coming but he could not wait for Sir Thomas to die.

Whatever the reason, Cromwell did not have to wait long. From our secular point of view, it was luck. Sir Thomas had died childless but that was never inevitable; had he been widowed, he would have remarried quickly and possibly produced heirs. Life was precarious, and inheritances were unpredictable because life was. Perhaps Cromwell saw the hand of God in this turn of events, or more accurately, a favourable judgement by the Almighty, as all events – good and ill – were His work. These events seem to coincide with his new, stronger, religious beliefs. We don't really know.

What was his new life like? It was an improvement. This failing cadet branch of the Cromwell family was back, at least to the same point as a generation earlier. One of the properties inherited was a house in St Mary's Street, Ely, where his mother was born. It was a substantial but unprepossessing half-timbered house, almost 300 years old when the Cromwells moved in. He became a lay rector and collector of tithes with an income of £400 per year; he had now almost equalled the yearly income of his late father, Robert, who had about £500 per year. He may have regarded it as home, unlike St Ives. His St Ives children were sent to Huntingdon for baptism; his last child Frances was baptised in Ely in 1638.

The downside was the location. Ely was associated with Oliver's family, but in the seventeenth century it was remote compared to both Huntingdon and St Ives. Ely, the centre of the Fens, was an inaccessible and modest place to live. When, later in his career, Royalists called him 'Lord of the Fens', it was not a compliment, referencing both his outrageous social pretensions and modest geographical origins. Ely had been the home of Hereward the Wake, one of the last resistance fighters to William the Conqueror in the eleventh century. Hereward managed to disappear deep into the fens and was never seen again. It was, literally, a backwater.

The landscape has changed considerably since the seventeenth century, much more than other parts of England, due to the drainage that had started before Cromwell's time. Ely was not like Huntingdon, despite the geographical closeness. It was the land of smaller houses, smaller horizons and smaller differences between the rich and the poor. Cromwell was now a bigger fish in a smaller pond; not that these relatively poor people would eat lots of fresh fish.

'Ely' is derived from 'Eels', and there were a considerable number of these in the flooded land around the town, which was a set of islands surrounded by damp marshland and rivers. The eel, thriving in the tidal marshes, was the standard diet of the poor. When you visit his former house today and enter the kitchen, one of the first things you see is something that has been beheaded – but it is an eel, not a monarch.

Cromwell's House in Ely is now a museum open to the public. It focuses on what life was like for a middling gentry family like his in the 1630s. The only other place in the UK where you can pay to see a place Cromwell called home is Hampton Court Palace, where he lived two decades later, in the splendour of a residence designed for the ruler of Britain and his family. The difference between the two homes really highlights the fact that the rise of Cromwell was the most rapid in British history.

The house consists of eight modest rooms. One of them, now branded as 'Mrs Cromwell's Kitchen', gives an excellent social history of food and food preparation – and it would certainly have been both mundane and time-consuming. This may seem an odd thing to do, when commemorating the life of one of Britain's greatest soldiers and politicians; it all seems a little pedestrian. However, it does remind us once again how far the Cromwell family had risen and how much abuse Elizabeth Cromwell received as she rose with her husband.

The homely recipes on display in the museum are interesting and popular with the visitors, but they come from a book (written safely after the Restoration) called *The Court and Kitchen of Elizabeth, Commonly called Joan Cromwell, the Wife of the Late Usurper*. The very simplicity, the use of locally sourced foodstuffs which seems so appropriate and even on-trend today, was designed as a satirical weapon against the Cromwell family. We have few verified pictures of Elizabeth – there is one in the Huntingdon museum – but the most well known comes from the hateful cookbook.

The book condemns 'Joan's' inability to spend money on feasts and her general parsimony. When she was living in Hampton Court, Royalists mocked her interior design plans – she was prone to dividing large palatial rooms into the type of cramped accommodation that she was used to in Ely. In the seventeenth century, the poor and powerless scrimped and saved; the rich and powerful took what they wanted from anywhere in the country. The Royalists made their point with food. Their propaganda claimed that she kept her own cows in St James's Park to save money. On one occasion, when the Protector called for a sauce for his loin of veal, 'Joan' replied 'that oranges were expensive now, that crab [Seville] oranges would cost a groat, and, for her part, she never intended to give it.' Other Royalist propaganda accused Elizabeth of drunkenness and adultery – the accusation of whoredom was never far below the surface when women claimed power above their 'natural station'. These never stuck because they were clearly untrue, so the fall-back position was her 'sordid frugality and thrifty baseness', which proved she had no right to rule: 'She was a hundred times fitter for a barn than a palace.' The husband was a king who was not a king, but Elizabeth had the added burden of being a pretend queen to a usurper.

The museum has a dilemma. Should they focus on the ordinary life that would have realistically occurred in this solid but relatively modest country house, or should they focus on the greatness of Cromwell as the Lord Protector? They do both, of course. The struggle for the tourist pound is very competitive. Cromwell is seen in the house with pen and paper in hand, clearly considering his responsibilities as Lord Protector; this did not happen. In the kitchen, Mrs Cromwell is seen at her embroidery; this probably did happen.

There is also a deathbed scene in the bedroom – an inaccurate one, as Cromwell died in Whitehall Palace in 1658, and there is the inevitable ghost story to bring in the customers. The new, on-trend escape room, with the focus on the paranormal, and the other compromises are designed to ensure an enjoyable visit for everybody. The Cromwell beer on sale in the gift shop is not a compromise; Cromwell drank beer. He had no objection to drink; for the sinful it brought their sins to the fore; but a Puritan, aware of the importance of his immortal soul at all times, could chance a beer now and then.

Cromwell lived in this obscure part of England even during the civil war itself. Ely was near the centre of his military operations for the first few years, so was as convenient as London. He returned to see his family regularly between periods of military action, but his family may have been only his third priority after war and politics. When Carlyle did his tour of 'Cromwelldom' in 1842 he noticed that the family home was near derelict and had earlier been a public house.

Cromwell would have been worried and angry at religious and political events during his time at Ely. There had been no Parliament since 1629. The Stuarts had no money to help Protestants abroad; the suspicion was that they wouldn't have done so even if they could. Charles I's influence would have borne down heavily on Oliver Cromwell through the king's main representative in the Fens. This was Bishop Matthew Wren, who arrived in Ely in 1638, after thoroughly alienating the godly folk of very puritan Norwich by driving through the king's religious reforms, suppressing the kind of independent preachers that we know Cromwell supported during his time in St Ives. The Archbishop of Canterbury, William Laud, was the well-known anti-Puritan powerhouse, but at the time Matthew Wren was not far behind in notoriety. The year of his arrival was the year that Cromwell acknowledged his new religious convictions, which did not include respecting bishops.

So Cromwell would have been no fan of Bishop Wren; he would have hated being overshadowed by the established church; his modest house was 300 yards from the cathedral and 400 years of continued rule by bishops would be a daily reminder that his views were out of kilter with the ruling establishment. While Cromwell and Wren were at Ely, sports were encouraged on Sunday, sermons were shortened and churches were more richly decorated. Cromwell would have hated all of this.

He was still an insubstantial figure, even in his own family. Sir Thomas Steward was buried in the cathedral. There would have been no plans to bury this Cromwell there. It was not even a Cromwell that was responsible for their current prosperity. It was the established church and members of the family on the maternal side that restored Cromwell's status.

Considering Cromwell's later conflict with the crown, the biggest conundrum was his passivity. His lack of action looks odd in comparison with the man of action that emerged after 1642. While other people, such as his cousin John Hampden, were protesting about Charles's new taxes, Cromwell was silent. He also worked for the Dean and Chapter, collecting tithes on their behalf. His world was dominated by the established church. He was not a soldier but a middle–aged tax farmer with seven living children by 1639. He was not likely to go off to fight for the beleaguered Protestants in Europe; the truth is, even if he wanted to take part in the great affairs of state, he was too old, too poor and too obscure to make a difference.

Cromwell did have some influence in Ely though. He opposed the draining of the Fenland, or more specifically, the bad deal that was given to the local land users by the king's drainage companies. This did not make him a Radical. There is no evidence that he was ever opposed in principle. He remained throughout his life a social conservative who harked back to a society that emphasised the responsibilities of the rich towards the poor as much as their privileges. Cromwell eventually achieved a twenty-year pause in the draining of the Fens, not by local activism but by the more drastic method of moving the country towards civil war.

The weakening of Charles I's power started when Cromwell was at Ely. The early revolt against Charles started in Presbyterian Scotland in 1637, after Charles's heavy-handed attempt to converge the religious practices of his two kingdoms. It looked like popery to the Scots. The king was unable to finance the subsequent war and when the Scots invaded England, Charles called a Parliament to raise the money to fight back.

For many Puritans, Presbyterianism was the natural step forward for their puritan dissatisfaction. Presbyterians wanted to replace bishops appointed by kings with locally elected church elders. They would enforce discipline and religious conformity. Scotland was essentially a Presbyterian country, on which James I (as James VI of Scotland) had grafted a set of bishops, to much popular disgust.

When the 1640 Parliament was called, it was English Presbyterians like John Pym and the Earl of Manchester that pushed through the reforms that triggered the civil war, with the victorious Scottish army standing menacingly behind. It was the Scottish army's interventions in 1643/44 that tipped the balance in favour of the Parliament, in exchange for which they received a promise of a Presbyterian Church in England.

For men like Cromwell who feared people like Wren, this change in religion was an obvious next step. However, Cromwell was not a Presbyterian. He objected to the Church of England as it was, but also rejected the Presbyterian alternative. Neither gave enough scope for the individual conscience. As a Puritan, he had no objection to controlling people's behaviour, but neither bishops nor church elders were the way to do it. Cromwell, unusually among the early leaders of the civil war, believed in religious toleration. It was that belief that was to make him loved – and reviled – later.

Chapter Six

God – Always Guiding Cromwell's Footsteps

Oliver Cromwell was an inconsistent human being. At least that is how he looks from our perspective. He was a king killer who essentially became a king himself; he was a religious man who organised war and killing with an efficiency and relish that we find chilling today; he was a miserable Puritan who put restraints on others that he did not always follow himself. 'Cromwell the hypocrite' was the view that was established soon after the Restoration in 1660. It has never gone away.

There *is* a way of bringing consistency to the man's actions – but we need a tool to decipher him that few people use nowadays. Oliver Cromwell cannot be explained without God. He was with Cromwell all of the time; whether Cromwell was in Parliament, on a battlefield or with his family, God was always there. No place, person or event was more influential; you cannot follow Cromwell's footsteps without Him, and you cannot make sense of his apparently erratic and changing behaviour unless you accept that in the seventeenth century it was not odd to have a personal relationship with God.

Despite the family's best efforts with his education, Cromwell seemed to have made his own mind up about the exact nature of his faith. In the 1630s he had a spiritual crisis and was what we might call 'born again'. Cromwell's 'extreme' puritanism does not seem to peak until the middle of his life, in the early 1630s, between his residence in St Ives and Ely. The Cromwell who resurfaced after this event was a different man.

Cromwell had always been a pious Puritan. He was taught that the kind of Protestant church created as a compromise by Elizabeth I was not the finished article – it was not pure enough, hence the name. Puritans did not like the status quo and thought the direction of travel was wrong. All were opposed to the religious changes of Charles I, seeing the newly beautified churches, elaborate rituals and new prayer books as evidence of creeping popery.

Cromwell never had any love for the authority of bishops and archbishops. On the matters of day-to-day practice of faith, Cromwell would be opposed to the power of the episcopacy. One of the changes that failed to happen to the Elizabethan Protestant church was the abolition of bishops and archbishops. Many European Protestant churches had abolished them, but they proved useful for English monarchs to help them enforce their wishes. Cromwell had a pre-crisis track record here. In the 1629 Parliament he criticised the power of Bishop Neile of Lincoln, who, Cromwell claimed, was misusing his power.

The genesis of the religious crisis is unclear. In September 1628 Cromwell consulted a doctor in London about his erratic moods and was diagnosed with melancholy. In the five years after, there are plausible stories of Cromwell being moody, slothful and unpredictable. When he moved to St Ives he converted all of his assets – bar 17 acres – into cash, and became a modest tenant farmer, which could be regarded as an erratic act. Given that he had already been drummed out of Huntingdon for his bad temper and behaviour, there does seem to have been the making of a crisis here.

He persisted with his life in England, despite considering emigration to the Netherlands or New England. At some unknown time there was a spiritual awakening and this was complete by the time he was in Ely in October 1638. Cromwell, in a letter to a relative, describes his religious conversion. He had been transformed from 'the chief of sinners' who 'hated godliness' and 'lived in and loved darkness' into 'a man rescued by God'. This letter has been used as evidence that Cromwell was a dissolute and rowdy youth. Cromwell's correspondence does admit to gambling, when he returned the £30 proceeds to the loser on the basis that he had committed a sin. There is little other evidence that does not come from hostile sources.

However, Cromwell's 1638 letter is talking about something much bigger than sins like gambling. He is describing the type of ignorance that somebody outside a state of grace would have, bemoaning a religious deficit of his whole personality rather than referencing specific events. It was common for those that we might call 'born again' to exaggerate their vices before their new state of grace. John Bunyan, a Puritan later persecuted by the Charles II, who would have had much less time in prison if Cromwell had ruled for longer, did the same in *Pilgrim's Progress*; the same phenomena can be seen in US television evangelism today.

Cromwell would have believed that his conversion could only be the work of the Almighty – certainly not his own – he was a sinner! God would also have done this for a reason. Cromwell may have believed he had been picked by God as a servant, selected for a special purpose, one yet to be revealed by prayers and signs. It was a theology that encouraged both agonising doubt and euphoric certainty, depending on the perceived state of your soul. Throughout his life, Cromwell experienced both highs and lows, rooted in his belief that almighty God was constantly monitoring him. On his death bed in 1658 Cromwell was still agonising about his membership of the 'elect'.

Cromwell's God was an active, judgemental one. So there had to be a godly reformation of manners based on the Bible. When Puritans like Cromwell took power after the collapse of the monarchy in the 1640s, that is exactly what was attempted. From a distance of 400 years, we gaze back at people who put the soul's salvation above everything else, and call them killjoys. If they could look forward to our time, they would be aghast that we seem satisfied with a single life followed by oblivion or imperil our soul with hedonism. Cromwell's reputation as a hypocrite comes from his minor personal failure to obey some of these strictures. In his defence, his devotion to his family, his love of practical jokes, his regular habit of drinking, smoking and chatting with his friends just made him more human. Perhaps he hasn't been forgiven for having principles different to ours.

Cromwell has two conflicting reputations – one for brooding, gloomy sloth, doing nothing for weeks or months and coming to decisions at the speed of a glacier, and another one for rash, impulsive action, no matter what the consequences to himself and others. How could he manage both? The answer lies with his relationship with God. His faith privileged personal conscience over everything else; his aim was to do God's will. This involved 'waiting on the Lord' for a sign, and later watching for further evidence of God's judgement on his actions and those of others. Cromwell was a man of action, but not before he was convinced of his own righteousness, and that was a long theological wrestling match. As a military leader he was never guilty of procrastination, as the thinking had already been done.

The next contradiction is Cromwell's use of God as a rationalisation for war. In our more secular age, there is not much credit in referencing God and even less in claiming to be His instrument on earth. Cromwell's reports back to Parliament contain as many mentions of God as military tactics. Comments about God being responsible for the victories and deaths of enemies sound terrible to us in the twenty-first century. In our individualistic, 'selfie' age, many would like him more if he had attributed success to his own talents; but God did it. This is a typical sentiment:

> Truly England and the church of god has had a great favour
> from the Lord, in this great victory given us.'

After the Marston Moor battle, Cromwell wrote a letter to his brother-in-law Valentine Walton. Cromwell reports that Walton's eldest son, Valentine, had died after the battle. It is a remarkable mixture of the personally empathetic and the religiously fanatical, and it causes some dissonance for people today, as we are far keener on the former than the latter. It contains the heartfelt transmission of the bad news, with the added detail that the parent probably needed:

> Sir, God hath taken away your eldest son by a cannon shot. It
> broke his leg. We were necessitated to have it cut off, whereof
> he died.

This was followed by a personal note that proved Cromwell's ability to understand the shock and grieving with a reference to the death of his own son, Oliver, earlier that year:

> Sir, you know my own trials this way; but the Lord has
> supported me with this.

And then he provides some consolation:

> There is your precious child full of glory, never to know sin
> or sorrow any more.

These are attitudes we can understand today; you do not have to be religious to understand that a faith can bring consolation. But then,

Cromwell's sentiments become a little more alarming, at least from a twenty-first century point of view:

> A little after [the amputation] he said, one thing lay upon his spirit … he told me that it was, that God had not suffered [allowed] him any more to be the executioner of His enemies.

This sounds like the fanaticism of the suicide bomber; or at least a Christian whose hatred has made them forget the sixth commandant. But Cromwell approved and expected the boy's father to approve, or else it would not have been part of this sensitive letter of sympathy.

This sad story is the second part of the letter. He starts with a euphoric and slightly bloodthirsty description of victory, ascribing success to the Almighty:

> An absolute victory obtained by the Lord's blessing upon the godly party principally. God made them as stubble to our swords.

Whether Cromwell was a military genius is a regular debating point among historians today. Cromwell would have been horrified by the presumption:

> Give glory, all the glory, to God.

How could such a social conservative organise the execution of a king? God is the answer again. Cromwell's decision to push forward with the execution of the king was made very reluctantly, very late in the day and not by him, but by Him. Cromwell was still supporting the existence of a form of monarchy led by Charles as late as 1648. It was clear that the victory of the Parliamentary armies in 1646, led by his instrument Oliver Cromwell, was a sign from God. By starting another civil war, the Royalists and their Catholic allies were in direct conflict with God's judgement against the monarchy.

Cromwell gains his negative reputation for condoning the murder of civilians, but his actions would have been rooted in religious belief. Firstly, the very existence of war and other calamities would be the result of sin. War was one of the ways that God showed his displeasure – both Royalist and Roundhead believed this. Cromwell would have noted the difference between the vengeful God of the Old Testament and the peaceable carpenter's son in the New, and the strictures of the sixth commandment, but war could still be justified. When Cromwell quoted from the Bible after a battle, it was always the Old Testament. In any war there would be a side looking for justice and an evil side. The side that lost – shown in their defeat – would not be automatically entitled to mercy. They had sinned, and lost God's grace. As shown in the relevant chapters, both the Basing House and Drogheda defenders had broken the conventions of war – further evidence of their perfidy. This made it easy for Cromwell to be relaxed, to use the modern term, about outrages which happened but he did not order.

This kind of belief was not merely a convenient theory for the victors. Charles I never forgave himself for allowing the execution of his advisor Strafford, and saw his own difficulties as a judgement from God, although he never doubted that He would look upon the monarchy with more favour, but perhaps not in his lifetime. That prediction was correct.

Part Two

SOMEBODY

Chapter Seven

Man of Action 1642–1644
Edgehill
Marston Moor

Cromwell was on the road to obscurity in 1640. He was a 41-year-old with no achievements of note and was approaching late middle-age by seventeenth-century standards. He had followed the same well-worn path of people who never entered the history books at all – the local grammar school, university, some useful law education and then an arranged marriage that was meant to benefit two families rather than fulfil the hopes of two individuals.

There were no signs of greatness. He was reduced to the status of a farmer feeding chickens in St Ives, and it was a fortuitous inheritance that allowed him to prosper in Ely. The first four years of his life in that tiny settlement were modest and uneventful. He seemed to have reached the highest point in life that people like him could expect. He was a substantial figure in Ely, but only as a large fish in the small pond that was the Fens.

People like Cromwell – discontented with Charles's religious and political policies and concerned enough about the consequences to risk civil war – were certainly needed to make the conflict happen, but there was no reason to believe that Cromwell would lead it. There had been no evidence of either leadership qualities or risk taking.

In 1640 he was one of the two elected burgesses for Cambridge. Among his own political class, he was a relative nonentity when he first arrived. He had a local reputation as a man who defended the rights of the poor from those who would drain and enclose the land that they had traditionally used to graze their cattle. His speeches against the king's religious and political changes were noted, but he was seen as a man of passionate words and emotions rather than action.

There were only 300 seats in the House of Commons and Cromwell was elected to one of the most prestigious. There is some confusion among historians about how he managed to do this. It seems that the Cromwell family's link with Robert Rich, Second Earl of Warwick helped; and by coincidence or not, Cromwell's solid stance against the king's religious and political policies was exactly what the earl required. Although Cromwell was well connected, he was still a peripheral figure. It was possible to be both.

Cromwell already had a track record of being ineffective in the Commons. As a Member of the 1628/1629 Parliament, his only known intervention was to support his teacher Thomas Beard. Cromwell recounted the story of a sermon by a Dr William Alabaster which Beard had described as 'flat popery'. The Bishop of Ely ordered Beard to respond to the errors of this sermon but the Bishop of Lincoln, Robert Neile, charged him with disobedience when he did so.

It would have been an insignificant anecdote even if had been current – but the story was a decade old. That's all this ruddy-faced provincial had to contribute. The delivery did not go down very well either. It was, in the words of John Morrill, 'stale beer', although it was followed up by more senior members of the Commons who were hunting around for examples of how Charles and his bishops could not be trusted with the Church of England.

Cromwell already had his diagnosis of melancholia, unimpressive parliamentary record, and fading family fortune. In 1640, he was heading towards historical footnote status. Yet in 1642, this inert nonentity turned into a man of action. Cromwell proved his impatience by starting the war even before the war. He was increasingly active in Parliament and was identified as one of the group lead by John Pym who wished to use the king's weakness to reduce his political power, and therefore negate his influence on the church. Cromwell's revenge on Wren came early in the proceedings. In December 1641, Wren was one of the bishops accused of heresy and by the next year he was in the Tower of London. He spent fourteen years there, longer than almost anybody else during the civil war, and longer than any bishop. He lived until 1667, and prospered under Charles II. His nephew was to design the new St Paul's Cathedral.

On 5 January 1642, Charles tried to arrest five members of the Commons who had opposed him most strongly, thus making the break between the king and Parliament complete. Cromwell was not one of them, but may have been if the event had happened a few months later. On 14 January, as part of the panic and anger, it was Cromwell who put forward the motion that the Commons should raise an armed force – 'in a posture of defence'. He was still using the moderate language of reluctance that would have appealed to the majority of the MPs. He was new to politics, but he was good at it.

It was war that made him famous, not politics; it was his success in war that made him a famous politician. He had despaired of the grandiose talk and posturing of his fellow MPs quite early in 1642 and was one of the first people to act as if war was going to happen, operating around his base in Cambridge. As early as January 1642, when no armies had been created, Cromwell took and reinforced the castle at Cambridge. The motte and fragments of earthworks still survive as Castle Mound and are open to the public. Cromwell then seized money and the university's silver plate that had been destined for the king. In July 1642, a month before the formal outbreak of war, the House of Commons journal recorded that Cromwell was arming and training the people of Cambridge. Had a political settlement been reached at this late stage, Cromwell would have been politically isolated and an ideal scapegoat for a treason charge, as a forceful but socially insignificant troublemaker.

Very few Members of Parliament – either on the Royalist or Parliamentarian side – actually risked their neck to be the first to initiate organised violence. War zealots, even obscure ones like Cromwell, were vital to turn military stand-off into war. A week after Charles had raised his standard at Nottingham in August 1642, and while other less impulsive people were still pondering the implications, Cromwell raised a troop of horsemen in Huntingdon. The choice of his original home rather than St Ives or Ely shows that he was recruiting volunteers on the real, albeit diminishing, power of the family name.

This is how the indolent Fen man became a whirlwind of political and military action. While he came to conclusions at the speed of a glacier, when convinced of the righteousness of the cause – God's cause – he would act very quickly and with a military skill that nobody could have guessed he possessed. Cromwell's righteousness also manifested itself in an outpouring of physical energy. His eleven years of remarkable physical and political activity have rarely been surpassed by anybody in Britain. It is lucky that Cromwell loved horses, as he would have spent a lot of time looking at their necks. In 1657, when a deputation arrived at the Banqueting House to make him king, he was waylaid by the chance to visit a recently acquired Barbary horse. Even in later centuries, when transport was easier, nobody covered the miles that Cromwell did.

There is no other British historical figure that requires a gazetteer of the British Isles to help understand their significance.

Despite arriving late at the first major pitched battle, at Edgehill, Warwickshire, in October 1642, he learned about war and formed conclusions about how it needed to be fought. The result of this battle was a draw, with the king's forces having the edge; but this was also a tragic result, as it ensured that the war would continue, as the bloodshed hardened hearts sufficiently to stop either side seriously seeking peace. Both sides even suffered the same number of casualties – about 700 each.

The Royalists may have won at Edgehill if Rupert, the king's nephew, had managed to do more than lead one glorious cavalry charge and then plunder the Parliamentary baggage train. What was needed, clearly, was moral and military disciplined leadership that was only gained by fighting for a cause you believed in. To Cromwell, that sounded like Cromwell.

Cromwell was also a little clearer than most about war aims; a man who started the war almost before everybody else was unimpressed by the Parliamentary watchword of 'For king and Parliament'. The fear of a treason charge still had power, and many Parliamentarians believed that the main point of the conflict was to bring the king back to the negotiating table in a slightly weakened position. The sight of Charles I on the actual battlefield disheartened and alarmed some soldiers on the Parliamentary side. The theory of the 'king's two bodies' was created as a result of these worries. Most convinced themselves that they were fighting the foolish, badly advised king in order to re-instate the legal, just, one. Cromwell rejected this idea from the beginning.

The word 'pitched' in the term 'pitched battle' implies some planning beforehand. This would include an agreed starting time. There is a myth about Cromwell, perpetuated by Hollywood, that he was present at the start of the Battle of Edgehill and was so frustrated by the negotiated start time that he ordered an attack before 'the appointed hour'. This did not happen, but it was designed to be shorthand for his impetuous bravery and refusal to adopt a gentlemanly attitude to war, both of which would turn out to be true in later, more crucial battles.

A visit to the Edgehill battlefield is a little less satisfactory than other civil war battlefields which are, rightly or wrongly, regarded as more significant. Much of the archaeology has been destroyed, ironically, by later military development and some of the battlefield is owned by the Ministry of Defence and access is limited.

It is possible to visit the free exhibition in St Peter's Victorian church in the village of Radway. In the church there is a National Heritage Lottery funded permanent exhibition called, controversially, 'The People's Struggle'. This interactive visitor exhibition is adjacent to the battlefield. It has information boards; artefacts, films and interactive displays which explain the events of the momentous battle and relate the impact it had upon the ordinary people of Radway and the surrounding area. For those who think that the battle might have been romantic – and we have the Victorians to thank for that image – there is a display of various sizes of cannon ball and the obvious damage they could do. For most of the enlisted soldiers at Edgehill, the sound of these lethal weapons being propelled through the air would have been the loudest noise they had ever heard in their life.

The exhibition is a convenient base from which to explore the battlefield, the surrounding landscape and this historic village. There are marked public footpaths that go up and across the Edgehill escarpment where the fighting happened. The Battlefield Trust has also published a walk through the area. It follows the route of King Charles, but still shows the places where Cromwell was.

1643

This was Cromwell's first year of national importance. He had the advantage of being both politician and army officer. In the winter months, when war became impossible due to the weather and the state of the roads, he was a politician. In the warmer months, he became an increasingly important member of the parliamentary army. Not everybody was as keen as he was. Some parliamentarians could see no way of defeating the king completely, and envisioned serious social consequences even if they managed it.

That was never Cromwell. It was Cromwell, more than other parliamentary leaders, who pushed for a total military victory. He wanted total defeat of the king before any negotiations could take place – this was not, of course the same as removing or replacing the king or the monarchy. Cromwell was not a republican–not in 1643, anyway.

Cromwell's historical reputation is linked inextricably to his methods of recruitment for his army. By 1643, he was in a position to recruit whomever he wished into his Eastern Association Regiment of Horse.

He had five troops of horse in March 1643; that had doubled by September. He was gaining a reputation for recruiting men of puritan conscience with a fierce desire to defeat the king – men in his own image. It is at this point, during the period of his popularity among modern liberals and progressives, that he gains his credentials for promoting on merit.

The quotation is famous, and slightly over-used, 'I had rather have a plain, russet-coated Captain, that knows what he fights for, and loves what he knows, than that which you call a gentleman and is nothing else'. This has become a universal popular sound bite. Everybody is in favour of promotion on merit. The phrase has been used with approbation on training courses at Royal Sandhurst Military College. It is a popular nostrum at business school and is a badge of the progressive-thinking meritocrats everywhere.

However, this is not exactly what Cromwell was saying. Cromwell was not disparaging the gentry, or doubting their pre-eminence – as the next, less familiar, part of the quotation shows 'I honour a *gentlemen* that is so indeed'. This apparent egalitarianism is very limited – these principles apply only to winning the war and protecting the protestant religion against Charles.

Cromwell was only a social progressive in the sense that he would mine the lower strata of society for recruits; his determination to win meant that he would look anywhere for devoted soldiers. He would appoint the sons of gentlemen; he took money from the poor Puritan women of Norwich to finance his eleventh troop. It had limits. It did not include (in theory), Anabaptists, who denied baptism, although it seems that some people with that belief were members of his troop.

The word 'Anabaptist' does not have a clear meaning to us today, apart from sounding like Baptist, a modern mainstream Christian group. The word implies 'baptised again'. Anabaptists rejected child baptism without a full affirmation of Christian belief. Some sixteenth-century groups, such as the radical Anabaptists of Munster, Germany, had briefly abolished money, introduced polygamy, smashed up images in the cathedral and introduced extreme puritan rules and compulsory adult baptism.

Sometimes Cromwell would deny that some recruits were Anabaptists, and sometimes he would say that it did not matter. 'Sir, the state in choosing men to serve it takes no notice of their opinions, if they be willing faithfully to serve it'. It would be another two centuries before that view became accepted by the majority.

> My Troops increase. I have lovely company. You would respect
> them did you know them. They are no 'Anabaptists' they are
> honest sober Christians; they expect to be used as men.

Cromwell's open recruitment of the 1640s was to serve him well for the
whole of his military career. He nurtured talent and reaped the rewards
later. One of many examples is Robert Swallow, the former commander of
the famous 'Maiden Troop' of Cromwell's original Ironsides, raised from
Norwich. At the Battle of Worcester (1651) Swallow's ferocious attacks
on the Presbyterian Scots was one of the turning points in Cromwell's
victory.

Cromwell's break with tradition was mostly real, but limited. He could
be as socially conservative as any member of his class. Favouritism was rife,
but this was not the word people at the time would have used; nepotism
was a natural part of life. When Cromwell was in a position to hand out
commands to his first five regiments, his 'meritocratic' choices were
Whalley (his cousin), Desborough (brother-in-law), Oliver Cromwell
(his son), Valentine Walton (nephew) and Henry Ireton (his friend and
future son-in-law). They would not have been appointed if they were not
competent; but this is not a meritocracy.

Cromwell has a reputation for both religious tolerance *and* religious
intolerance. Our modern view tells us that they cannot exist at the same
time within the same person. For a man who was part of a movement that
would not blink at the murder of Catholics, Cromwell's reputation for
religious tolerance seems unmerited. It still does not seem like religious
toleration to us today. Our toleration must include the unencumbered
right to practise a religion different to our own, as long as neither actions
nor beliefs jeopardise public order.

Cromwell could not manage that. His religious toleration did not
extend to Roman Catholics, who by definition were a danger to civil
society, although those who later lived harmlessly under his rule were as
free from persecution as Catholics under James I. Neither did Cromwell
feel able to tolerate, in principle, two other groups, both Protestant. He
offered little leeway to those who supported the Protestant church of
Queen Elizabeth with over-mighty bishops, Catholic-feeling ceremonies,
and the fear of more popery in the future. He had no love for the Scots,
even when they were helping him win battles, which they certainly did,
especially at Marston Moor in 1644. He disliked Presbyterians almost

as much as Royalists. Presbyterians were struggling to replace bishops, not for the freedom of conscience for all Protestants. Cromwell once famously said that he was not wedded to any specific form of government, but perhaps more importantly he did not feel the need for a rigid form of Protestantism.

Most of Cromwell's men were still the sons of middling gentry, but the number of social inferiors was also remarked on. The Presbyterian Earl of Manchester noted it – the same earl with whom Cromwell had clashed about the rights of poor fenland farmers. Cromwell, with his precarious social status, his refusal to panic when independently minded Protestants disagreed, and his first hand knowledge of the poor but principled fenland Puritan, was fighting this war differently – and to win.

With his new type of soldier, Cromwell moved like a whirlwind through his own region in 1643, consolidating East Anglia, Essex and Hertfordshire, while at the same time neutering the importance of the king's garrison at Newark. In January he secured his own constituency of Cambridge and in March foiled a Royalist rebellion in Lowestoft. In April and May he secured Lincolnshire for Parliament by securing Crowland Abbey near Peterborough, and then secured Grantham and Stamford in the early summer.

On 28 July 1643 the Parliament took, or more accurately re-took, Gainsborough from the Royalists, led by the king's grandson Sir Charles Cavendish. Cavendish made a mistake that was to be made again and again in the war – the belief that the Cromwellian cavalry would not return to the field after an attack. Cromwell, aided by his brilliant second-in-command, James Berry, defeated the Royalist force and ensured that the town could not be used as a base to harass Parliament in Lincolnshire. Berry was said to be responsible for the death of Cavendish himself, a man who had made Cromwell's life difficult. Berry, whose first job was as a clerk in a Shropshire ironworks, was to rise to be one of Cromwell's Major-Generals during his protectorate. He was promoted on merit and his willingness to kill the king's close relatives in battle – two qualities that even some of grandest members of the Parliamentary army did not possess.

Cromwell had now secured his part of England for Parliament and blocked the opportunity for the Royalists to march on London. In July 1643 he was rewarded by being appointed Governor of Ely. In October 1643, he fought with Sir Thomas Fairfax for the first time at the Battle of Winceby. This was one of the first predominantly cavalry-based battles of the civil war. Cromwell was not able to contribute a lot as his horse was shot dead under him at the beginning of the battle; by the time he had found another one, the victory was Fairfax's. The battles in this part of East Anglia seemed insignificant at the time; they were nasty skirmishes that produced death and injury without materially affecting the course of the war, but they were occasions when the Parliamentary horse were superior to the Royalist horse. That would be vital later on.

By autumn of 1643, with war being logistically difficult as the weather deteriorated, Cromwell spent his time in Ely and at Westminster, where he was on the Committee of the Two Kingdoms which formulated the war policy. He was a key political player and an important military leader – advantages that his friend Fairfax and his enemy the Earl of Manchester never had. It was increasingly noted, especially by Cromwell, that the Southern Armies were doing less well under the leadership of the Earl of Manchester than his Eastern Association.

1644

When the conflict continued into 1644, Cromwell was fighting outside East Anglia, moving further west in the areas between London and Oxford. He managed to push forward to the walls of Oxford and in January 1644 became second-in-command to the Earl of Manchester, a man about whom Cromwell harboured severe doubts. He was back in Parliament in mid-January to mid-February 1644, when the war paused because the weather made it impossible. Four years earlier, Cromwell had been minor gentry under the shadow of the Bishop of Ely; at the beginning of 1644, he turned up at the cathedral himself to issue demands – calmly – about how the service should be conducted.

The main concern of 1644 was the increasing success of Prince Rupert, who was threatening to lift the Parliamentary siege of York. Cromwell's fame and success meant that he was now operating outside his traditional eastern base, and it also meant his fame had spread to the opposition. They were the two most celebrated cavalry leaders in the land by 1644. Rupert was probably more aware of this than Cromwell. When their armies met at the battle of Marston Moor in July 1644, Rupert asked if Cromwell would be present; Rupert saw the battle as two egos and reputations contesting each other. When Cromwell heard about Rupert's enquiry, his response was much more wearied: 'By God's Grace he will have fighting enough'.

Despite Cromwell's lack of interest in personalising the fight, it *was* personal. The result of this battle would mean the destruction of at least one reputation. Rupert had never been beaten, and Cromwell's success meant that he was regarded by others not so much as a lucky charm, as that would be superstitious, but as a holder of God's grace. 'It was observed God was with him, and began to be renowned' said Joshua Sprigg, Thomas Fairfax's chaplain.

Apart from being essentially unbeaten, they were opposites who had nothing in common – age, experience and attitudes were all different. Prince Rupert had suffered greatly for the Protestant religion. His mother, King Charles's sister, was Elizabeth, briefly Queen of Bohemia until Catholic forces displaced her husband in 1620. Rupert, who was born in Prague, knew the danger of Catholic resistance much more than Cromwell. He was at the siege of Breda in 1637 when Cromwell was merely grumbling about bishops, and spent three years in an Austrian prison, made longer by his refusal to renounce his Protestantism. All this by the age of 21.

One crucial thing they did not have in common was the ability to obey orders. Rupert, in his euphoria of success after York and his youthful ambition, chose to deliberately misunderstand the king's written order not to engage the rebel army after his initial success. By Saturday 2 July, both armies were arraigned against each other in the fields between Long Marston and Tockwith, five miles west of York. The weather was terrible, many on the Royalist side were not ready and Rupert was outnumbered by about 10,000. Cromwell's armies rarely engaged unless they had numerical superiority, and the numbers in this case were very unpromising for the king's army.

The morning and the afternoon passed without much incident. There was some half-hearted Parliamentary artillery fire and more enthusiastic psalm singing in the cornfields, but nothing had happened by 7pm and Rupert went for his supper. It was a sensible move; Rupert understood the concept of a surprise attack – he had been planning one himself. But now it was late; it was a wet and thundery summer day with only a few hours of unreliable daylight left. It was July, the corn was high and wet and it would have been very difficult to be fighting on foot. It was then that the Parliamentary forces attacked; a collective decision of the leadership, with Cromwell at the fore. It was rash, reckless, and a success.

Cromwell made two vital contributions to the victory. He initiated a successful cavalry charge at the start, and rescued the battle at the end by wheeling round to support Thomas Fairfax's troops who were in danger of being defeated. He sustained a neck injury that took him out of the battle for a time – a reminder of how the course of history can be changed by a bullet or a pike one inch in a different direction.

It was a close-run thing; so close that early reports of the battle proclaimed a Royalist victory. Cromwell would have found it difficult to defeat Rupert without the help of the Scottish allies – about whom Cromwell was wrongly dismissive in his reports back to Parliament, causing deep offence and continuing suspicion. Not all of the Parliamentary forces did well that day – although Cromwell's letter of 5 July made it clear that the victory was the work of his godly men 'saving a few Scots at our rear'.

Marston Moor made Cromwell's reputation. From then on he was 'Ironsides' and by extension, so was his army. However, victory at Marston Moor was not followed up properly and the king not yet defeated, but the main northern army had gone. Rupert had also been stopped in his tracks. It was going to take one more major battle to defeat the king militarily, although that would not be enough to defeat him politically.

Today the battlefield is well preserved and its exact location is secure. Long Marston and Tockwith have not expanded very much in the ensuing 350 years and the road that ran through the middle of the battlefield is still there. They are enclosed rather than open fields now, and the burial place for about 4,000 soldiers in the biggest pitched battle on English soil. Human remains were still being found two centuries later. Nearby was the bean field where Rupert hid, and his poodle Boy was killed by Roundhead soldiers on suspicion of having Satanic powers. On high ground there is a tree cluster called Cromwell's Plump (sometimes Clump) which, despite its name, was the starting point for Fairfax's soldiers and a surveillance post. There is an obelisk erected by the Cromwell Association in 1939 and the site has the usual interpretation boards.

Chapter Eight

Victory and Vengeance 1645
Naseby and Basing House

If you follow Cromwell's footsteps to the Naseby battlefield, near Market Harborough in Northamptonshire, there is no doubt where the battle took place. Although the location is certain, the topographical changes caused by housing, enclosure, farm building and new canal and roads has transformed the landscape, so some imagination is needed when considering how the battle was fought.

Naseby was the place where the Royalists learned to treat Cromwell and Fairfax's New Model Army with respect and fear. Up to this point it had been a joke – 'the New Noddle Army', as the Royalist Commander Lord Digby sniggeringly styled it. The contempt of Charles's advisors, more interested in jockeying for their own position, eventually convinced Charles to take on an enemy that outnumbered them. Even Prince Rupert, brave and often reckless at Marston Moor, was doubtful about this tactic.

While the Royalists bickered over tactics, the Parliamentary side was much more disciplined. The chain of command was reasonably clear- the Commons was in overall charge, with Fairfax the commander on the ground and Cromwell his deputy. When, in May 1645, the Commons ordered Cromwell to manoeuvre himself between the king and Oxford, and the Parliamentary forces to the East, he obeyed the instruction without complaint, although he did not agree. He always accepted his instructions from Parliament – his biggest rebellion was no more than the passive-aggressive begging letters, praising his army and asking for money to look after them.

Cromwell was cheered enthusiastically by the soldiery when he and Fairfax were reunited in June 1645 and Fairfax insisted that Cromwell became second-in-command. They were an impressive pair. Fairfax's own tactics had forced the king into a position where either a fight or a hasty retreat were the only choices, and Cromwell had collected 3,000 horsemen from Cambridge. It was always teamwork that won the day for Parliament.

Naseby was a victory for the philosophy of Cromwell and his Puritan soldiers and the last failure of the 'devil–may–care' Royalist approach, personified once again by Rupert. Rupert's method was to intimidate Cromwell's army by an old-fashioned cavalry charge. It worked at first. The Royalists gained the upper hand, as the Parliamentary foot soldiers in the centre wavered and fell back. Unlike Rupert's men, who could attack only once, Cromwell attacked successfully the Royalist left wing and then regrouped and attacked the Royalists from behind.

Edward Hyde, later the Earl of Clarendon, was a hostile commentator on the New Model Army , but noted that their discipline extended beyond Cromwell's command. All cavalry regiments would charge a second time, while the Royalists could seldom be persuaded to rally again to consolidate any initial success.

Rupert could be of no service. He and his men had ridden away to plunder the Parliamentary baggage train rather than regroup after the first charge. While his men were piling up treasure on earth, Cromwell's soldiers were ensuring victory. It wasn't just religious fervour – it was military efficiency. The watchword was 'God and our strength' – that's two things, not one. By the time Rupert had returned, large numbers of foot soldiers had surrendered and the cavalry, making a rational decision, refused to charge. One side just wanted to win more – that same side would regroup and fight again whether they were winning or losing. In 1865, the military historian Robert Neville Lawley got the point exactly: 'The Royalists never seemed to have learnt, till too late, that a pitched battle is not a hunting day.'

Cromwell was convinced that his army of protestant toleration, having essentially won the war, now deserved the fruits of victory. He told the House of Commons this in a letter: 'He who ventures his life for the liberty of his country, I wish he trust God for the liberty of his conscience'. The Presbyterian-dominated House of Commons published all of Cromwell's correspondence except this part. Problems were accumulating that would lead to conflict within a few years.

The king was now defeated militarily. His last useable army was smashed. His reputation was also destroyed by the capture of his private correspondence, which proved that he would have countenanced Irish Catholics being recruited to his side. Naseby also ushered in a new era of incivility, with the murder and mutilation of the women following the Royalists baggage train. They were mostly wives of army officers and camp followers and some of them would have been prostitutes, but they all had their noses slit and faces slashed all the same. It was mostly the work of the Parliamentary foot soldiers, not the New Model, but it was a horrible indication of how the war was going.

There is a monument near the entrance of the battlefield which marks the spot where Cromwell's cavalry began the engagement. Interpretive boards give details of the battle and a second monument explains the battle and its consequences. There is at the moment no battlefield museum or study centre here. It deserves one. Its importance as a turning point in British history should put it in the same bracket as Hastings or Bosworth Field.

The proposed site for the battlefield museum is All Saints church, Naseby. The plan is to have a visitor and community centre in part of the church building while maintaining it as a place of worship. The church has a link with Cromwell; a seventeenth-century table stands in the north aisle, said to have come from the now demolished Shuckburgh House, which is opposite the church. It was believed that after killing some Royalists who were eating around the table, Cromwell's soldiers went on to eat their own meal there.

Naseby Battlefield Project has created an excellent battlefield trail and wishes to do more. The feeling is not new – Thomas Carlyle, in search of Cromwell the hero, visited the site and bemoaned the fact that there was nothing there except bits of bone under the soil. The nineteenth century rumour that Cromwell is buried on the battlefield is exactly that.

The war continued. In autumn 1645 his New Model Army swept from Bristol, going eastward to London via Devizes and Winchester, taking the town on 5 October and then on to the destruction of the Royalist stronghold at Basing House, Hampshire in October 1645. That was another turning point, both in the war and attitudes to it.

Those members of the British ruling class, like Cromwell, who gambled on civil war in 1642, could not claim that they had not been warned about the possible consequences. There was a central European war of religion taking place, mostly in Germany, whose name suggests its unrelenting nature – the Thirty Years War; 8 million died in that conflict. Many of the horrors of the war were mirrored by similar events in Britain; one that wasn't was the siege, and the British Civil War would have been a lot worse if both sides had been unable to break sieges. The historian John Barratt estimates that there were over 300 sieges in cities, towns, castles and manor houses during the civil war. If they could not have been broken, then the civil war might have dragged on for many more years.

One major example of a civil war siege is Basing House, Hampshire. The name is misleading – it is not a house but a castle ruin. When you visit the site itself, the old fortifications and medieval earthworks can still be seen, with the remains of New Basing House, which was completely destroyed after the siege finished. It is clear that it was a castle before it was a house – originally with a towered gatehouse protected by a dry moat. In the words of the website, 'the nationally important historical ruins of the largest private house in Tudor England, which suffered at the hands of Oliver Cromwell during the English Civil War'. 'Suffered' is an understatement. It was reduced to rubble, first in an attempt to storm it, and then as a deliberate policy to eradicate it.

Basing House was the biggest private palace in the country when it was built; it was visited both by Henry VIII and his two daughters. Mary I went on honeymoon there with her Spanish, Catholic, husband Phillip II in 1554. Elizabeth I visited as well, but then the tight-fisted monarch made a habit of this everywhere. The owner during the civil war was John Paulet, Marquis of Winchester, a Royalist and a staunch Catholic. Basing was called by its defenders 'Loyalty House' – not to the king, but more infuriatingly to some, to Henrietta Maria, his Catholic queen.

Cromwell's determination to take it was heightened by religious hatred. Cromwell described Basing House as 'a nest of idolatrous papists'. This spacious home had been besieged twice before Cromwell arrived and had suffered two and a half years of intense fighting. It was also a target of Puritan hatred, exacerbated by the arrival of an all Catholic garrison, put there on the marquis's insistence and the king's agreement in 1645. This weakened the defence just at the time when the Parliamentary army were in a stronger position to take it.

Basing House also held a strategic position controlling access to London, and the Parliamentarians had long coveted it. Cromwell was not at Basing House for very long. After the fall of Bristol he swept eastwards to finally mop up the last Royalist resistance on the road to London. He had been in Devizes and Winchester in September 1645 and only arrived at Basing on 8 October. The image of Cromwell riding through the country from one victory to another sometimes obscures the amount of work done by others, especially in the area of artillery, which was usually responsible for quick victories in sieges. Hugh Peters, Cromwell's bloodthirsty chaplain, noted with satisfaction that a hole had been blown in Winchester's walls in less than a day.

It was, as ever, the Parliamentary war machine, not one man, that achieved the victory. In late September the house was being bombarded, with part of the fortifications being destroyed. Poison gas was used; brimstone and arsenic had been added to wet straw and set alight in another example of 'total war'. All that was needed after that was force of numbers and the bravery and fanaticism to push through the breaches that would soon be made in the walls. So, morale and defences had already been damaged before Cromwell arrived with the leadership, bravery and 7,000 fanatical soldiers who stormed the house on 14 October, in a clash that lasted between one and two hours.

Once the walls had been breached the result was inevitable. In the archaeological remains, defenders' bullets have been found that were never fired because they had panicked when loading their weapons. There is still much to be found underground in the places where the Victorians failed to disturb the ground and there are still regular archaeological digs on the site.

Something else was destroyed on that day, not for the first time, but decisively, and that was the civil war's reputation for civility. No offer of 'quarter' – the right to surrender without further punishment – was made to the defenders. In fairness, the brave Marquis of Winchester did not ask for it, so it will never be known for sure if Cromwell would have granted it. It seems unlikely.

A few defenders escaped death, including Inigo Jones, who had been sent to Basing House by the king to improve its defences. Four Jesuit priests were killed and others taken away to be executed elsewhere. The women there were relieved of their clothes but not killed or abused. Other defenders were burned to death in the fire that later destroyed the building, but not before it had been plundered. It was now the type of conflict in which fellow Englishmen would be stripped of their fine clothes before being buried. Cromwell would have condoned such tactics.

These events were part of an increasing intolerance of Irish fighters, or indeed anybody from Ireland. There were hints even before the siege that they were in trouble. A local newspaper reported:

> It is hoped that they will imitate their neighbours at Winchester Castle and accept of fair terms in due time before it is too late, for otherwise, many of the garrison being papists, they are like to receive little favour from the besieger.

There was now a prevailing ethos in favour of cruelty, one that Cromwell did not create, but also had no moral scruple with. Cromwell was therefore unconcerned when Catholic soldiers and civilians were killed during and after a battle or a siege such as Basing (or later, Drogheda). He uses the language of God's approval which sounds alien to modern ears:

> This is a righteous judgement of God upon these barbarous wretches, who have imbued their hands in so much innocent blood.... (Drogheda, 1649)

The Siege of Basing House makes Drogheda easier to understand. They both show what the policy of 'No Quarter' means in practice when mercy had been drained from both sides by the accumulated hatreds of civil war.

In the same way that Cromwell receives the plaudits for a victory organised by others, he also gets the obloquy for the murderous consequences – the murder of Catholics – but Cromwell was but one of a movement who were now prepared to use any form of violence against the religious enemy. Supporting Cromwell was John Pickering's Regiment. Pickering was a religious radical who had learned his trade in the Eastern Association, just like Cromwell, and led soldiers who shared his view. He lead the furious attack on Basing House and the treatment of the enemy, and in Pickering's men, Cromwell 'had willing executors of his order' (John Barrett, *Sieges of the Civil War*).

It was the fire and the slighting of the house that created the ruin which can be seen today. Once all the moveable goods had been stolen, Parliament passed an ordinance allowing anybody to take away the building materials. Cromwell had asked the Commons to destroy it, as it would pin down around 800 men to defend it adequately (he had stormed it with only 300 inside), and that the damage done already made the building unviable as a defence. It was the prime example of a 'ruin that Cromwell knocked about a bit', as the song goes, but this needs to be seen in perspective. Cromwell destroyed nothing after a battle without the permission of a vengeful Puritan Parliament. Many of the other places that claim to be Cromwell's victims were the result of vengeance of other military leaders. He was no worse than most – just more infamous.

Basing House is well worth a visit, but as befitting the greatest private house in the country at the time, there is a strong walking element. There is a 7-mile trail through the grounds and the town (The Basing trail), but it also offers shorter versions. There are interpretation boards which explain the historical importance of the ruins. There are two audio tours, on the Tudor era and the English Civil War, which can be downloaded before any visit.

The only intact building is a huge tithe barn, built is 1535 and the location of much bloody fighting in an earlier siege, when Sir William Waller, with less fanatical troops (some even mutinied and went home) and no siege artillery, failed to take the house in 1643. You can see the cellars where a group of defenders were trapped and tragically killed during Cromwell's assault in 1645. At the time it was called the 'Bloody Barn'; now it is licensed for civil weddings, which sometimes affects the ability to visit it. Cromwell would have been too perplexed to be angry at the thought of marriages being performed in a warehouse, and of a former sacrament becoming a secular ceremony.

There is a lovely representation of the house in Lego at the entrance, and a small museum with the results of some of the archaeological digs in the ruins. Like many of the civil war locations in this book, the attractions become even more interesting when the Sealed Knot is there doing one of its famous re-enactments. The Sealed Knot – a family-friendly hobby with a keen interest in history but no religious and political bigotry – is one of the best things that came out of our bloody civil war.

Less than half a mile from the house is St Mary's Church in Old Basing. It suffered during the civil war, like many churches occupied by Cromwell's 'godly army'. It was a victim of the army's shortage of material and hatred of Catholic images. Seats, pews and pulpits had been burned to make space for horses. Lead was stripped from the roofs and from the tombs of the Paulet family. Their remains were scattered around. It seemed that the soldiers did have the time to write the names of the bodies that they had exhumed in chalk on the walls. Statues of saints and images of the family were destroyed and there are still bullet marks scarring the walls. A statue of the Virgin Mary seems to have survived because it was covered with ivy. The church was further ruined by the attempted restoration of 1660.

The ghost of Oliver Cromwell has been spotted (again) around Grange Farm, by people liable to see ghosts. Like other places in the ghostly footsteps of Cromwell, they are all as haunted as you want them to be. If the ghost of a person hangs out in places where they experienced fear or regret, there should be no reason for a Cromwell spectre to be there. He was absolutely certain that what he was doing was right.

Chapter Nine

Very Reluctant Republican 1646–1648
Putney

The Presbyterian minister Richard Baxter had severe doubts about Oliver Cromwell and the New Model Army. Baxter felt compelled to join as a chaplain in order to tackle the terrible attitudes that he encountered among the soldiers. They were discussing religion and politics, pressing forward their own opinion and considering those of others, and generally celebrating the lack of religious uniformity. It was clear that their leader shared their attitude, and it was this army that won the civil war, not the one that the Presbyterian rebels put together in 1642.

This was not even Cromwell's regiment, but that of Edward Whalley, future gaoler of the king at Hampton Court, regicide and republican, who avoided the king's vengeance in 1660 by escaping to America. Cromwell was not the only man whose thinking was changing – the events of 1649 would not have been possible if it was.

Some of the soldiers at Naseby alarmed Baxter because they called for the end of the monarchy or the punishment of the king. Cromwell would have parted company with them at this point. It took a long time for increasingly dismal events and appalling kingly behaviour to turn Cromwell into a reluctant and temporary republican and regicide.

On one side were people like Cromwell, the kind of people who rejected both the king's version of a national church and the Scottish Presbyterian version favoured by many in Parliament, known as Independents. These soldiers, who had travelled outside their parish, were still able to worship God effectively. They now felt they could live without a rigid structure of parish church, government approved preachers, bishops or strict Presbyterian elders. Religious expression had become a personal choice.

Parliament shared Baxter's suspicions. But it was an English Puritan army that had handed victory to the MPs, and this contained Protestants of all sorts, not just Presbyterians. Under the command of Fairfax and Cromwell they had defeated the king by 1646. Usually, when armies win, they are thanked and sent home with pay. The MPs decided that they should be told off, given no more money and sent to Ireland. The army were also horrified that, even after the king's defeat, the MPs were still trying to negotiate an easy settlement with him, one that his duplicitous behaviour and defeat in war did not deserve.

Even those who were not so 'puritan' were fighting for a cause. It was clear to all that it was they who had won the war, not the MPs, and they wanted something back. For most, it was back pay and immunity from prosecution. For others it was religious toleration. In June 1647, with the king in the hands of the Parliament and the MPs about to betray the soldiers, Cornet George Joyce captured the king on behalf of the army. Cromwell was behind this attempt to seize the political initiative, although he was not present when it happened.

At this point, Thomas Fairfax still agreed with Cromwell. The army, said Fairfax, were much more than,

> mercenary soldiers, brought together by the hopes of pay and the fortunes of war; the peace of our country, our freedom from tyranny, the preservation of due liberty, the administration of judgement and justice, the free course of the laws of the land, the preservation of the king, the privilege of parliament, and the liberty of the subject, were the main things that brought us together.

None of these events created Cromwell the temporary republican. He was still a social conservative when he convened a meeting to discuss the future governance of the country in October 1647 at a church in Putney. He had no choice but to discuss future constitutional arrangements, and the settlement with the king, with 'extremists' in the army.

Cromwell had partly created the embarrassing situation he was in. The officers that confronted him – called Levellers by their enemies – had a power base in the New Model Army that Cromwell had created himself. It was an army that had been conscripted without thought of rank and many of these members had a strong puritan conscience which meant they actively wished to defeat the king. By November 1647, the emboldened officers of these men were demanding a share in government for those who had sacrificed themselves for the cause that had been won.

The Church of St Mary the Virgin on the banks of the Thames at Putney is a major landmark in British political history – and we have precious few of these. It is not the place where British democracy was actually born – that was later, and was the work of many people in many places – but it was where democracy was spoken of explicitly for the first time. More significantly, the debates broke the fixed idea that the way a country was run had already been decided by God and kings. A new, 'from scratch', written constitution was suggested for the first time.

Modern British politics started here, and the church still holds regular debates and exhibitions on the subject, while still being a working parish church. If you visit the church, you are able to stand in the same places the debates took place and follow Cromwell's footsteps, or more accurately, the place where he did a lot of grumpy shouting. His presence at the debates did not mean he was a democratic man of the people. He did not believe in the kind of parliamentary democracy that we have now, despite being given the credit for its development by his admirers today. He wanted a government for and by the people who held property. He did not look forward or wish to plan new constitutions – he wanted a return to a similar type of governance that existed before a bad king ruined it.

What was Cromwell's political philosophy?. There was a clear difference between ruler and ruled. You governed, or you were governed. The only thing that the lower orders deserved was to be governed fairly, but that did not mean having a say in the way it happened; they were merely to trust those who had been directed by God to rule

However, these are not Cromwell's words. They are the last words of Charles I on the day of his execution at the Banqueting House a mere sixteen months later. Cromwell had arranged drummers to drown out his words if necessary; the crowd were anyway quite far away; but it wasn't necessary, as the king's last speech was uncontroversial. There was nothing here for Cromwell to disagree with, apart from the last part. The king, by not behaving like a king, had lost the right to be one. However, both men shared an utter contempt for democracy.

By late 1648, Cromwell had changed his mind about the situation, but during the Putney Debates of October 1647 he still worked for a settlement with the king within the old framework. He did not want to be at Putney and he certainly did not want to chair the meetings. Fairfax, his superior, was suffering from a diplomatic illness; he did not like the topics that were about to be discussed either.

Cromwell was clearly still a supporter of monarchy – in theory – when he reluctantly convened the meeting in late October 1647. He was still ready to negotiate with a defeated king, and the Levellers and many in the army could not understand this position. On 20 October he had made a long impassioned speech in favour of the institution of monarchy in principle and the Levellers were well aware of his position.

Cromwell opened the meeting with a request that everybody should speak freely – a sign that he knew that the real power was in his hands. They took him at his word. Some Levellers and army leaders had already reached the conclusion that there was no settlement possible with this king. One of them, Edward Sexby, commented peevishly on the first day that they had 'laboured to please a king and I think, except we go about to cut all our throats, we shall not please'. Many were unimpressed by Cromwell's continued attempt to find a settlement. Your 'credits and reputations have been much blasted' continued Sexby. Sexby knew Cromwell's reputation as a fighter – he had been present at Naseby, but this was politics now.

It was inevitable that Cromwell and the Levellers would clash at Putney. There was a fundamental difference between Cromwell and Ireton and the Radicals like Sexby – 'The Levellers were attempting to shut the door on any return of the king and the Cromwellians were seeking to keep it open' according to historian John Lees.

Leveller demands varied, but they wanted to extend the right to vote (for men only – Putney was not the home for democracy for women), increase the power of the Commons with elections every two years, and reduce or abolish the power of the monarch and the House of Lords. As well as a share of power, these Levellers wanted a new, more democratic constitution for Britain. They had written down their demands in a document called the *Agreement of the People* – essentially Britain's first written constitution. Cromwell did not believe in any of this. He had fought the civil war to make the king behave, not to abolish the office, but he had no choice but to listen because the victorious army contained a powerful, organised minority of army officers and civilian supporters who wanted these things – and the army had won the war. While Leveller ideas were in the minority, it made political sense to hear their views.

Why Putney? At that time it was a town of less than 1,000 people about 4 miles from London. It was the headquarters of the victorious army, and the army had chosen it as their base because it was near enough to make the point about army power, and far enough away not to be too provocative. Accidentally, it was also the birthplace of Cromwell's distant relative by adoption, Thomas Cromwell, when it was even more rural. This was the Cromwell who was laughed at by the Tudor courtiers for being the son of a brewer, and now his relative was the main power in the country. Some of the powerful army agitators opposing him in the church had been brewers, cobblers and shop keepers.

Today, the church is a place of pilgrimage – assuming that is theologically possible – for left-wingers and Radicals who believe democracy was born there. However, the Putney Debates were not held in a church by accident. The religious element needs to be remembered. Cromwell, as chair, started the thirteen days of meetings with a prayer – a day's worth of calling on the Lord and reflection. None of these political Radicals so beloved by the modern left would have complained; they took part enthusiastically, although it seems that Cromwell, who was clearly stalling throughout the whole debate, may have welcomed a lengthy prayer session more than most.

Cromwell and his son-in-law Henry Ireton spoke for the army command – the grandees – against those men who wanted political change. One of the Levellers, Richard Overton, has left us his graphic view of Cromwell: 'You shall scarce speak to Cromwell about anything but he will lay his hand on his breast, elevate his eyes and call God to record … He will weep, howl and repent even while he doth smite you under the fifth rib.'

The main argument for more democracy was made by Thomas Rainsborough:

> I think that the poorest he that is in England hath a life to live,
> as the greatest he; and therefore truly, Sir, I think it's clear,
> that every man that is to live under a government ought first
> by his own consent to put himself under that government;
> and I do think that the poorest man in England is not bound
> in a strict sense to that government that he hath not had a
> voice to put himself under.

Part of Rainsborough's famous speech is written on one of the walls of the church; there is no mention of Cromwell's reply. Cromwell himself had first entered Parliament in 1628 with an electorate of twenty-four. He was totally contemptuous of Rainsborough's ideas. Democracy would bring anarchy.

The meeting ended after thirteen days when Cromwell told the officers to go home and 'conform to those things which were within their sphere', but there continued to be disquiet in the army, especially when Cromwell and Fairfax ordered an oath of loyalty to be taken. St Mary's is the place where Cromwell proved that he was more of a religious than political radical. He had no interest in the constitutional theory – he just wanted a political settlement that offered religious toleration for Protestants and maintained a weakened monarchy.

Much of the outside of the church remains the same – it has the same tower that was 200 years old when Cromwell saw it – but the inside has been altered by the restless Victorian 'beautifiers' and some deliberate vandalism in the 1970s, which had, some would say, similar results. There is still a corner of the church that can be identified as a place where the historic debate took place. There are medieval pillars and angels that Cromwell may have gazed on, as he wished the whole thing would go away, but tourists visit the church more for what it represents rather than the building itself.

A visit can do more than soak up the atmosphere, however. The *Guardian* has taken an interest in the church as a site of political importance. Indeed, the *Guardian* and its readership are still debating how Britain should be governed today. Since 2007, the newspaper has funded a permanent exhibition with digital copies of the debate transcripts, explanations of the civil wars, and details of seventeenth-century Putney from the archives at Wandsworth Council. There is also a historical commentary on the meaning and legacy of 1647 by civil war historians such as Tristram Hunt. The exhibition attracts visitors from abroad with an interest in democracy as a global rather than a national phenomenon, especially US citizens who also like to trace the events in Putney to the origin of their democracy at home.

Some visitors have suggested that the exhibition has too much emphasis on religion, but as previously stated, the first day of debate was actually a long prayer session, and every subsequent political point was backed up with evidence from the Bible. Even the most radical Levellers from the time would probably have been shocked by the contents of any modern edition of the *Guardian*.

There is another very important exhibit – a verbatim report of the three days of the debate that was kept by William Clarke – some have called him the real hero of Putney. This is our source for the democratic discussions and Cromwell's reactions to them. However, they did not come to light until they were discovered in Worcester College, Oxford in 1890. By this date many men had the vote and although this was essentially what the Levellers were asking for in 1647, clearly a lost manuscript could not have been very influential on the growth of the franchise in Victorian times.

It was not the high-blown legal and political arguments of the Levellers that convinced Cromwell that the king had to be removed. It was Charles's own behaviour. Charles was enjoying the emergence of this new force opposing Cromwell even while imprisoned in Hampton Court, but he also worried that frustrated members of the army would try to murder him, something which Cromwell took active steps to prevent. He was still not in favour of regicide, formally or informally.

Two days after the dissolution of the meeting, the king escaped from Hampton Court and the civil war began again. Sometime between the escape and the end of the second civil war, Cromwell changed his mind about even attempting a settlement with the king and adopted a more radical position. The second civil war turned Cromwell into a reluctant and temporary republican. Ireton, his co-conspirator at Putney, went in the same direction. In the theatre of God's judgement, Charles and those who supported him were working against the Almighty. By restarting the war, he was ignoring God's judgement implicit in his defeat in the first one. After the second civil war it was the army that decided that he had to go; when Parliament continued to talk to the king after a second civil war, their patience snapped.

On 18 October 1648, Ireton worded a petition to Parliament 'that the same fault may have the same punishment in the person of the king as in the punishment of the poorest commoner'. The army were calling the king, 'Charles Stuart, the man of blood ... the man against whom the Lord had witnessed ... let the safety of the people be the supreme law'. Cromwell threw in his lot with this army towards the end of 1648. These changes of mind did not mean that he accepted the democratic ideas of the Levellers. The Levellers, and the agitation in the army, was a problem that was postponed until the fate of the monarchy had been decided.

Thomas Pride, a brewer before the war, played a large part in the eventual execution. On a cold December day in 1648, it was Pride who stood with a group of musketeers outside the House of Commons with a list of MPs that the army had decided to exclude from Parliament because they still wanted to settle with the king. Cromwell was perfecting the political skill of being absent when something contentious happened. Just like the capture of the king by the army a year earlier, he was behind the move. In war you have to be present; in politics it is often better to be absent.

The remaining seventy MPs – the 'Rump' as their enemies called them – went on to declare 'the people' as the source of all power (represented by themselves, obviously), abolish the House of Lords, try and execute the king, and declare England a republic. All this happened in six months. As Lenin said 'There are decades where nothing happens; and there are weeks where decades happen'.

Chapter Ten

Trials of Strength and Weakness
Westminster Hall, Palace of Westminster 1649–1653

Westminster Hall is open to visitors today as part of a tour of the Palace of Westminster, and is the only place in the complex where we can literally walk in Cromwell's footsteps. Cromwell's frenetic activity around the Palace of Westminster has mostly been erased by fire – in a literal rather than a poetic sense. The 'medieval' looking Parliament buildings that visitors see today were rebuilt after a fire in 1834, and the only major significant survivor is Westminster Hall. The Commons Chamber did not survive the fire, but the chapel of St Stephen occupies the same footprint as the old House of Commons between 1547 and 1834. During this time, the chapel was a mere 1ft wider than a singles tennis court and over 12ft shorter; this tiny room was meant to accommodate the equally tiny non-aristocratic ruling elite, although to be fair it was only in times of crisis that it was full, and then the conditions were intolerable.

Westminster Hall was the only building that survived the Luftwaffe incendiary attack of May 1941. Just as in 1834, a conscious decision was made to save this building at the expense of the two chambers. The building was rescued by Walter Elliot MP who ordered that the emergency services focus on saving the medieval hall – after all, as he remarked to a friend years later, they could always build a new Commons Chamber, while the hall was irreplaceable.

From 20 January 1649, The Hall (and the medieval painted chamber, demolished after the fire in 1851) was where the decision was made to try the king of England for breaking his contract with the people to rule within the law.

It was already a place associated more with justice than law making. Three of the main English courts – Common Pleas, Kings Bench and

Chancery, met there before and during the civil war. Treason trials had always performed there – William Wallace, Sir Thomas More and the man who had plotted to kill Charles's father, Guy Fawkes. Thus it made sense to set up a high court of justice and use Westminster Hall as the location.

It was one of the biggest buildings in the country at the time, and still feels huge today; then, as now, this feeling was increased by the removal of unnecessary fixtures and fittings. Pictures of it show stalls against the wall in normal times – it was as much of a shopping mall as anything else. This public trial was a declaration of the righteousness of their cause, and there were about 5,000 people crammed in the building during the trial. Members of the public were allowed in, even though partisan soldiers predominated.

The last time it had been used for a treason trial was the process that condemned one of the king's advisors, the Earl of Strafford, in March 1641. It was at the stage of the civil war when the Parliamentary opposition was still blaming 'evil advisors' for the political and religious actions of the king. A trial like this should have been held in the Lords, but just as for the trial of the king, a larger space was used to make a public display of Strafford. In any case, the Lords had been abolished by the Rump Parliament because they had refused to accept the legality of the whole process.

Despite looking similar to the trial of Strafford, it was different, and these differences show how much had changed between 1641 and 1649. The jurors would not act in 1641 if the king was officially present so he had to be hidden in a box at the back. In 1649 he was the accused party; in 1641 the Presbyterians were assaulting their king by proxy, but in 1649 more radical Puritans and army officers were attacking the king himself. One of the very few constants was the presence of Oliver Cromwell.

By 1642, Cromwell was merely one of the active war party who believed that the defeat of the king in battle was required before a political settlement could be reached. By 1648 he had realised that defeat in battle was not going to be enough, and that a public event highlighting his guilt would be necessary. That would be difficult. Support for the process was draining away almost as it was prepared, even among the instigators. A committee headed by Cromwell had drawn up a list of 135 commissioners to judge the king, of which a maximum of seventy actually turned up. Foreign powers were watching events with horror and alarm. Support for the king, even in London, was growing. Cromwell was taking a risk with this trial; one that we, in retrospect, tend to underestimate.

How had Cromwell got to this desperate point? Those who find Cromwell a hypocrite have argued that he always wanted to reach this stage, and to be fair, he had form. He was an enthusiastic early adaptor for war, mocked the early Parliamentary battle cry of 'For king and Parliament', and did once say that he would kill the king if he met him on the battlefield. This does not add up, however. What happened was that sometime in 1648, Cromwell decided that Britain without a king was a viable solution for a country at the end of its tether. Cromwell's enemies have accused him of organising a 'show trial'. That seems a little unfair, especially with its twentieth-century connotations of Joseph Stalin. It would be fairer to say that it was a process in which only one verdict was possible, but the final punishment was less predictable.

Charles's behaviour during the trial pointed to the root of the impasse. Legally speaking, he held all the cards. The Magna Carta ruled that people were tried by their equals and the king had none, on earth anyway. His judges were from Parliament and elsewhere, places that were not even courts in their own right; it was foolish to accuse Charles of breaking a contract with the people. Such 'contractual' monarchies did exist; but England was not one of them. They needed him; he was their king – they could not deny it. He told them all of this, with some scorn. These arguments had worked before, but lost their force now that Cromwell and people like him no longer accepted them.

Charles decided to attack the court's constitutional legality. Most of day two was spent in exhausting discussions about the legitimacy of the process. He was on strong legal grounds over the four days of his interrogation, but that was not going to save his life. The fact that the judge, on a platform with the commissioners against the High Window, was a relatively obscure Cheshire lawyer wearing metal sheets in his hat to avoid assassination did not enhance the dignity of the court.

Charles also played the snob, which may have made him feel better but did nothing to help him live. Sat on a dais in the middle of the Hall, surrounded by wooden partitions and rough soldiers, he refused to respond or remove his hat for the whole of the proceedings. Charles made it obvious that he did not recognise these people, either socially or legally.

On day three of the trial, the court removed to the Painted Chamber and took evidence without the king; they felt more comfortable going over old wounds, but the trial was not going their way as a public spectacle of justice.

Cromwell was now the main force behind proceedings. Fairfax, although named as a commissioner, decided that the trial was one step too far for him. When his name was called on the first day there was silence, apart from somebody shouting out that he had more 'sense than to be there'. This was Thomas Fairfax's wife Anne; in response she received the traditional rebuke from men when women tried to intervene in politics: she was called a whore by guard Daniel Axtell, and nearly lost her life in his violent overreaction.

The next day, Charles changed his tactics. He offered to appear before the House of Lords and Commons to answer the charges, which he had resolutely refused to do so far. In one way, this undermined the king's own position, that there was no legality of any kind in the trial, but it further embarrassed the commissioners. Some were desperate enough to consider the notion. Those like Cromwell, who had experienced the king's double dealings before, knew that he was prevaricating again. With the tide turning a little against the commissioners, it was a sensible idea for the king to try to 'buy time'.

It was Cromwell who put an end to it. On the Friday of the trial, John Downes, one of the commissioners and MP for Arundel – they did not call themselves judges – lost his nerve. When the king in his new slightly more conciliatory mood, suggested further consultations about the matter, Downes whispered to Cromwell that perhaps in the name of humanity, they should consider the king's request. 'Have we not hearts of stone?' he was reputed to have said. This was countered by Cromwell who doubted Downes's sanity.

Cromwell and Downes were relatively close friends; the main difference was that Downes had spent the civil war amassing a fortune by dealing with confiscated Royalist property. Cromwell put a rapid end to his tender feelings but Downes withdrew from the court, subtracting a little more from its credibility. Downes still signed the death warrant, however, and when the monarchy was restored was one of the many who claimed that he had been intimidated by Cromwell. In 1660 he swapped a grisly execution for a damp and nasty incarceration in the Tower of London for the remaining six years of his life.

On Saturday 27 January 1649, the British Republic was declared at Westminster Hall when a guilty verdict and an execution were announced. However, the Rump Parliament had failed to abolish the monarchy and any execution would merely lead to the automatic accession of Charles II. It was clear already that the new experiment had not really been thought through, beyond the removal of one man.

The Rump Parliament failed to rule adequately without a single leader. Fairfax had withdrawn from politics, Henry Ireton died in 1651, which left Cromwell as the head of an army that had defeated the Irish in 1649, the Scottish in 1650 and the Royalists in 1651. The re-instatement of rule by a single person and a Parliament in the form of Lord Protector took place on 16 December 1653, and inevitably Cromwell was that single person; equally inevitable were the cries of 'hypocrisy' from those who believed this had always been his plan.

Britain's first written constitution was formally ratified in Westminster Hall. It is an obscure document that deserves to be better known. The deeply pragmatic name: 'The Instrument of Government', has not helped to secure its place in history. It separated the power to make laws and the power to enforce them in a way that would have made Charles I faint; the new Protector's Council was like a King's Privy Council but with more power. Parliament had to meet every three years and ultimately would be able to overrule the single person, who had a contractual obligation to an elected body representing the people. Such a constitution did not exist in 1649, although it suited the king's judges to claim that it had. The only problematic point in this 'birth of democracy' story is that the plan needed the consent of a small cabal of army officers before Cromwell was able to consider it. That's not very democratic.

Cromwell was present at another investiture, as Lord Protector, at Westminster Hall on 26 June 1657, and the differences show the failures of the constitutional experiments since 1653. This time, there was an attempt to make the event as regal as possible. Instead of the plain black suit worn by Cromwell in 1653, he appeared in a robe of purple velvet-lined ermine. In front of the great window, in the approximate place he had sat just eight years earlier, he sat on the coronation throne of Edward I, which had been removed from Westminster Abbey. He was regaled with a sword, sceptre and Bible – but no crown.

The only thing missing was the word 'king'. The investiture of the Lord Protector lacked nothing in kingliness except the name. The desperate need for stability and a government that was recognisable meant that Parliament had actually voted to offer Cromwell the traditional title of king not the made-up title of Lord Protector. Cromwell thought about it for a month, changing his mind regularly, and waited on the Lord. Ultimately, he could not be convinced that it was what He wanted, and despite the support of Parliament, his key army allies were vehemently opposed. They threatened to resign if he became king; their influence was still immense.

Later, in 1661, Westminster Hall was the location of the symbolic burning of some of Cromwell's laws and was the obvious place to put the heads of Cromwell, Ireton and Bradshaw as a salutary lesson to regicides and usurpers; but from that point onwards, it would always be the place where the British monarchy was temporarily ended and permanently tamed.

Chapter Eleven

Execution 1649
The Execution Warrant
The Banqueting House

Although the execution warrant of Charles I is not literally a footstep, it was the greatest step taken by any individual in British history and is the most famous document of the English Civil War. The original is in the custody of Parliament – a reminder, perhaps, of who won the war in the end – but facsimiles are available in most relevant museums and their shops. It is ubiquitous.

By 1649, the government had been taken over by the army – it was a coup d'état – similar to the ones that we see on television today in countries we disapprove of. The attack on Parliament was condoned, organised and supported by Oliver Cromwell; this small, unrepresentative power then organised the execution of the king. To some people, this is another sign of Cromwell the bully.

This single piece of parchment is the most famous execution warrant in British history. It contains the names of the fifty-nine commissioners of the High Court who authorised the death of the king. The word 'commissioner' was deliberately vague and legally meaningless. In reality, but not in legality, they were his judges, with the verdict already decided. But this doesn't make the warrant 'fake news', as has been suggested. Two myths exist about the document: that it was completed by a bloodthirsty mob, which unthinkingly condemned their king without a moment's thought; and that it was the sole work of the evil Oliver Cromwell, who intimidated and coerced people into signing. The truth is less clear cut and more complicated.

Cromwell's name is not first or second on the warrant – but that is not the evidence for the defence. John Bradshaw was the judge at the king's trial; he was a second-rate lawyer from Cheshire who had been volunteered for the post in his absence and whose republicanism and ambition conquered his fear of assassination. The second name is Thomas Grey of Groby, a member of the House of Lords (recently abolished) whose prominent position was needed, pragmatically, to show wide support for the execution.

Cromwell's name is third. There are good reasons for this, without in any way reducing his importance. Cromwell was the leading force behind the trial and the link between the politicians and the army. He also stiffened resolve when others weakened on the last day of the trial. He was the one who would have pursued people with his pen to sign the warrant. He told one signatory, Thomas Waite, that 'these that have gone in shall set their hands. I will have their hands now.'

He pursued but he did not persecute. There is no evidence that those who confirmed the sentence of death but did not sign the warrant were harassed later. Nobody has ever claimed seriously that signatures were forged, although many of the other excuses made later were a bit pathetic. When the king returned, some of the regicides claimed that they had been forced to sign the document, but then they would, wouldn't they?

Many others refused to take part in the process altogether and no harm seemed to have come to them. Algernon Sydney, an implacable enemy of the king, told Cromwell a few days before the trial that the court he had set up was unfit to try any man, let alone the king. Sydney's credentials as an ally allow us to believe Cromwell's reply: 'I tell you we will cut off the head with the crown on it'.

What is less known is that Sidney changed his mind a year later; describing the act, a little ambiguously, as very 'brave', he continued to support the new regime.

Cromwell's comment seemed to prove that a 'not guilty' charge was impossible; the trial was designed mainly to stop the war. Charles had proved, to Cromwell's satisfaction, that as long as he was alive he would be a problem. In the December before execution, there had been one last attempt to negotiate with the king. His possible last chance was to agree to abdicate in favour of one of his children, whom Parliament would aim to control. By turning this down, Charles had more-or-less added his own name to the warrant.

Further evidence that the verdict was a foregone conclusion was the fact that signatures had been added to the document before the proceedings finished on Saturday 27 January. Many of the names on the warrant would need no encouragement; for others, some psychological pressure must have been applied, and that would have been done by Cromwell. Despite wanting signatures, it would be a mistake to think that Cromwell had a certain number in mind – it was God, not man, who was asking for this execution. A close look at the document shows rubbings-out and alterations as the date for the execution had to be changed; some have argued that this proves Cromwell could not risk asking the reluctant for a second signature on a fresh document. The truth may be more prosaic; it was the logistical difficulty of finding the people and the need to do it quickly. A domestic rebellion or foreign invasion was a real fear at the time, however unlikely it seems in hindsight. There was no time to lose.

Cromwell already had the power to do what he wished – he did not even bother to fill the single page, and, if anything, it looks like towards the end they were squeezing signatures in. It could be argued that they were leaving room for more, or the opposite: they clearly felt that they already had enough. Cromwell knew that he was in a minority, amongst humans on earth, anyway. When the Rump Parliament proposed the law to bring the king to trial (and formerly abolished the Lords when they opposed it) it passed by a pathetic twenty-nine votes to twenty six.

When the monarchy was restored in 1660, some of the regicides were prepared to say anything to avoid being chopped in four and castrated while alive. Robert Tichborne claimed that he was young and impressionable – he was 31 – nearly middle aged in the context of the time. Henry Smith's signature can be clearly seen on the top of column four but he could not remember signing it. Many blamed Cromwell. Richard Ingoldsby claimed that Cromwell had dragged him into the Painted Chamber and forced him to write his name by holding him down and putting a pen between his fingers. Cromwell must have done this with great sensitivity, as Ingoldsby's signature in column five flows beautifully. The truth is that it suited a lot of people for Cromwell to be seen as the psychotic bully responsible for the regicide.

Most of these men signed for their own reasons, some similar to, and some different from, Cromwell; most of these men thought long and hard about signing the document. John Hutchinson's wife Lucy reported that he only signed after serious prayer and reflection, coming to the conclusion that it was the will of God. This was the view of most, and some, like Edmund Ludlow and Henry Marten, were republicans who needed even less convincing. Both of these men eventually fell out with Cromwell when he later seemed to be insufficiently republican. Cromwell was by no means the most extreme of the regicides.

Most were proud of what they had done. Attaching their name to a public document and holding a public trial also showed that they felt they were in the right. In the last column of the warrant it seems that the name of Gregory Clement had been partially rubbed out. The story is that Clement was found guilty of adultery with a maidservant in 1652 and his name was removed by the Rump Parliament. This may not be true – he was still executed in 1660, and his name wasn't removed very well, but it does reinforce the idea that for the people whose names were attached, it was an honour that could be taken away.

The king killers signed the document for the nation's peace and under the instruction of God, who had clearly withdrawn his support from Charles Stuart. It was designed to bring peace to a country that was well and truly at the end of its tether. Afterwards, nothing in British history would ever be the same. There's nothing fake about the execution warrant – that's why it matters.

Banqueting House

Kings had been deposed and killed in British history before. In 1327 in Berkeley Castle, Edward II met a very painful death after an assault with a poker that left no evidence of external injuries. Richard II was starved to death in Pontefract Castle in 1400. Henry VI, another king who lost a civil war, was murdered in the Tower of London in 1471. Charles could have been killed or poisoned in a 'hole in the corner' way, and indeed one of the reasons for Charles's slightly unkempt appearance at his trial was a fear of allowing an army barber anywhere near his neck. None of these other killings were public events, so the very use of the Banqueting House marks a major, but uncelebrated, turning point in British history.

Some historians have described the events in Britain between 1640 and 1660 as the 'invisible revolution'. It may or may not have been a revolution but there is a strong claim to its invisibility. A visit to the Banqueting House in Whitehall does not give any indication that the only British Republic was initiated there, and even today, that element is not emphasised very much. If the Banqueting House was a historic building in Paris, the events of 1649 would be celebrated very differently.

Perhaps the nature of the building makes it easier to make it 'royal' rather than 'republican'. It was a glorious achievement of the Stuarts and gives an impression of what the buildings of the royal court would have looked like if the Stuarts had continued to run the country. It had been a recent addition to the monarch's palaces, started in 1619 and officially finished in 1622 with costly additions made at regular intervals until the 1640s. It was a complete, separate building without the maze of interlocking corridors of the rest of Whitehall. At the time it would have shone out as a modern building surrounded by the decrepit Tudor buildings that Charles would have replaced if his French-style, free-spending monarchy had continued. Had Inigo Jones's plans not been interrupted by civil war and lack of money, this new palace – with the Banqueting House at the centre – would be ten times bigger than Buckingham Palace today.

Today's building would be recognised by a traveller from Stuart times, apart from the whiter stone facade added by the Victorians. On the inside, the main difference is the people who look around it, often with their heads tilted upwards to examine the ceiling, painted to celebrate the greatness of the British monarchy. The original design by Inigo Jones left the great beamed ceiling with blank squares, rectangles and ovals, ready to take enormous decorated canvases that glorified the Stuart monarchy. The hall was completed in 1636, just before the monarchy that it celebrated fell apart. The final touches were made in March 1639, when the Scottish rebels struck and the disintegration of the Stuart monarchy began. The magnificent Rubens survived because it was on the ceiling and could not be removed and sold in the 1650s.

The building is a contradiction. It is a testament to both the divine power of kings and their destruction. The Rubens Ceiling was the work of both Stuart monarchs, mooted by James I and completed by his son. The subject was the divine right of Kings and depicts King James accompanied by angels on the way to heaven; it would have been one of the last things Charles would have seen before his own execution. Just before that he would have seen his own art collection up for sale at St James's Palace – apart from the overtly papist works which were ripped to pieces and thrown in the Thames. As the Victorian historian, Ernst Law, commented:

'Little did James know that he was raising a pile from which his son would step down from the throne to the scaffold'.

After the execution, the building changed its function. It was originally a place of eating and entertainment. Masques were famously held there; a sophisticated blend of poetry, propaganda, music, dance and outlandish costume, in which king and queen sometimes took part. It was the type of behaviour that enraged Puritans; apart from the fun and frivolity, women were acting on stage. During the period of their powerlessness, Puritans ranted and raved about the goings on in the Banqueting Hall. Some, like William Prynne, had their ears removed for insulting enthusiastic thespian Queen Henrietta Maria, when he compared women who acted to whores.

The Banqueting House was also the place where the courtiers partied while the Thirty Years War destroyed Germany and Protestants were in retreat everywhere. Charles did not have the money for an aggressive foreign policy but he did have enough cash for a good time with his friends. When smoke from the candles was damaging the newly installed Rubens, the king built a separate room for plays called the King's Masking House, and the Puritan Parliament had it destroyed when they took power.

Why was the Banqueting House used as the place of the execution? Tyburn was the normal place for the execution of traitors. Cromwell was to be humiliated there exactly twelve years later. No location was specified in the regicides' warrant, but the Banqueting House was ideal. Tyburn would have been a security nightmare; the execution of the king was not a popular move, but in the eyes of those who forced it through, it had to be a public spectacle of justice and emphatic proof that the power of the Stuarts had gone. So the execution had to be brazen and confident, but the problem was that most of the regicides were neither of those things.

The window was temporarily removed and replaced by a door to the scaffold designed to publicly execute Charles I, opening up into a Whitehall yard where people congregated. The reasons for this have been disputed, but it would have meant that the execution was taking place much above the heads of most of the observers rather than level with them. The actual window no longer exists as it was not in the main hall, but just outside it in an adjacent part of the building and would have been the next window along at the north end, roughly above the current visitors' entrance. It does seem that Cromwell was prepared for a negative reaction. The crowd were also a fair distance away and Cromwell had drummers available to drown out any unwanted speeches or crowd noise.

You can't see the exact spot where Charles was executed by peering at the windows, but there is a bust of Charles near to the 'Whitehall SW1' sign which marks the approximate spot. Where was Cromwell when this happened? It is hard to tell. Most – except Hollywood – agree that he did not witness the execution, but he would have been nearby, reflecting and praying. He probably did not see the event – but then, he did not need to. It was his work.

As the main attraction in the building is the art, it would be a good idea to use the audio guide in this museum, as Rubens' work, once you get past the magnificence, does not really speak for itself – the meaning has been lost over the centuries. There is an interesting introductory video in the undercroft. To avoid anything bad happening to your neck, like Charles Stuart, it is a good idea to use the bean bags provided. The genius is mostly on the ceiling

It was at the Banqueting House that Cromwell formally declined the invitation to be king in 1657, after ten weeks of agonising. He may have rejected the title of monarch, but the Banqueting House remained the place where the Lord Protector staged audiences with ambassadors from abroad and prominent British politicians in a monarchical style. It was built for a king's pleasure and to reinforce his godlike view of kingship; forty years later it was the place of business of a working republican leader, formerly a tenant farmer.

Part Three

EVERYBODY

Chapter Twelve

England's New Chains Discovered
Burford, 1649

The Levellers, who Cromwell met at Putney, were not happy with the turn of events in 1649. John Lilburne, a man who Cromwell had supported in the past, was now his implacable enemy. Earlier in the war, in 1643, Lilburne had moved to Boston to serve in Cromwell's Eastern Association. He fought with marked bravery at Marston Moor in 1644. He seemed to believe in liberty of conscience as much as Cromwell, but by 1647 they had parted company and 'Freeborn John' was in prison at the time of the Putney Debates.

Lilburne could not even support the execution of the king. He then made it obvious that he preferred the inept tyranny of Charles to the undemocratic rule of the Rump and the chairman of the Council of State – inevitably, Oliver Cromwell. In March 1649 Lilburne lamented the lack of real progress in his provocatively titled pamphlet *England's New Chains Discovered*.

> We were before ruled by a king, Lords and Commons ... now a General, Court Martial and a House of Commons, and, we pray, what is the difference?

Lilburne was ready to make it personal:

> O Cromwell! O Ireton ! How has a little time and success changed the honest shape of so many officers!

Violence was always an option to quell army mutinies. In the days after the Levellers had been dismissed at Putney in November 1647, there was a rebellion at Corkbush Field in Ware, Hertfordshire. Loyal soldiers were used to quash it, a declaration of loyalty to Fairfax was demanded and one ringleader, Private Richard Arnold was shot. This delicate operation – picking on one person to atone for the sins of the others – only works if the loyalty of the vast majority could be relied upon.

Cromwell knew the importance of looking after the soldiers, most of whom were more worried about arrears of pay and immunity from prosecution than creating a democracy. Cromwell, who had been sending letters to beg for money for his soldiers since he took up command, was still trying to do so now. Radical soldiers were a minority but Cromwell both feared and hated them. The numbers of soldiers supporting the Levellers are unknown, but probably in the thousands and Fairfax and Cromwell were worried about what would happen if agitation in the army continued and grievances were not dealt with.

On 9 May Cromwell was in Hyde Park making conciliatory noises on these issues to the vast majority of loyal soldiers but he could make no compromises with the 'sea green men' who were inciting rebellion in the army against an unrepresentative Rump Parliament. The Levellers did not want to go to Ireland – they had no interest in helping to set up another Cromwellian dictatorship there and no desire to foist Protestantism on anybody who did not wish it. There was less conflict here; for the same reasons as them not wanting to go, Cromwell did not want to take them.

In May 1649, there were rebellions all over the south west, starting at Salisbury with 1,000 breaking away and camping in the village of Burford on Sunday 13 May. The Burford rebels were expecting some kind of compromise to be reached. What they did not expect was a furious Cromwell covering 45 miles in one day and surprising them with 2,000 cavalry on Sunday night/Monday morning. There was a minor skirmish at the Crown Inn at the corner of High Street and Sheep Street where one soldier died, and that was the pretext for locking up 340 soldiers in the church and threatening them all with severe punishments for mutiny. About 800 men had escaped, so there needed to be some exemplary punishments which even those who had run away would hear about, and learn a lesson from. Those captured soldiers were crammed into St John's Church, Burford, where they endured two days of lectures and harangues on loyalty and godliness from Cromwell until the Thursday. The atmosphere was one of recrimination. It was widely believed that Cromwell had reneged on a promise that force would not be used against them, so when it happened, the sense of betrayal was even greater. He also rejected the request to discuss the Levellers' new manifesto, 'The Agreement of the People', after initially giving the opposite impression. The time for negotiation was over.

Cromwell did not spend nights in the church and, with hundreds of soldiers cramped into a small space in fear of their lives, it was a good decision. Cromwell spent his evenings at Burford Priory, an Elizabethan manor house. It is presently owned by family members of media mogul Rupert Murdoch. Then it was owned by William Lenthall, the Speaker of the House of Commons during the civil war, and the person Cromwell would report to with each military victory. Lenthall would remain speaker until removed on Cromwell's orders in 1653. He is buried at an unknown location in the church at Burford.

The house is about a five-minute walk from the church, and while it is not open to the public, it is worth a visit. It was built by Sir Lawrence Tanfield, whose tomb alongside his wife is one of the other attractions of the church, but one that divides opinion. Had Cromwell gazed on Sir Lawrence's tomb, he might have remembered that Sir Lawrence was an associate of his uncle in the early parliament of James I, at a time when monarch and subjects were able to make government work properly.

With nothing to think about other than their grievances and the threat of death, it must have been boring and stressful in that church. One of the prisoners had time to write a matter-of-fact plea on the lead-lined font that is still in the church. It is faint but clearly says 'ANTHONY SEDLEY 1649 PRISNER'. There is also a Nine Men's Morris board carved into one of the tombs – another way of passing the time.

Anthony Sedley would have worried for his life, but in the end only three ringleaders were selected for execution. The plaque to the 'democratic martyrs' can be seen on the south wall of the church. Cornet Thompson, Corporal Perkins and Private Church were shot, while the others were forced to watch from the roof of the Lady Chapel. Cromwell's victims are buried in unknown locations in the churchyard, but the bullet marks are still visible on the walls of the church. Cromwell then made the rest sign a grovelling apology and recantation of their views in exchange for their lives.

On the first day of the harangue, a Treason Act was passed by Parliament and there was a new crackdown on Radical publications and pamphlets. The Leveller movement was effectively over and their ideas were not rediscovered until the 1970s, when the plaque was put up by Labour MP Tony Benn and the Levellers were reinterpreted for the modern age.

St John's Church has become a place of pilgrimage for left-wingers in the same way as the church in Putney. Leveller Day is the nearest Saturday to 17 May, where the Leveller ideals of freedom, equality and religious toleration are celebrated and Cromwell is frowned upon as the man who strangled democracy in its crib. Burford is very much the place where the modern British left and Oliver Cromwell part company. At least during the debates in 1647 he pretended to listen and did not have anybody shot on the spot. This was not the case at Burford. It wasn't so much the token execution of ringleaders, which would have been expected – it was the total refusal to listen.

Cromwell and Fairfax spent some weeks after the events of Burford being fêted at All Souls College, Oxford, and were made Doctors of Civil Law in a city that had once fought harder than anybody to defeat them. Other military leaders were given honorary academic awards. In a reminder that Cromwell was not the only show in town in 1649, this joyful display of grovelling was called the 'Fairfaxian Creation'. There were equally elaborate celebrations in Westminster Hall by a Rump Parliament of about forty MPs and an army that now governed the country. They were clearly the new establishment, and the joy at Oxford showed genuine relief at the routing of the rebel Levellers. Fairfax and Cromwell ruled supreme in England. Cromwell's next step took him to Ireland, to the further detriment of his reputation but the enhancement of his power.

Chapter Thirteen

Bolting the back door
Drogheda and Wexford 1649–1650

Ireland is the place where Cromwell's footsteps resonate most today. His reputation for condoning cruelty worse than that already expected in warfare was achieved in a mere nine months in 1649 and 1650 – a remarkable if negative achievement, but not one that he achieved on his own. When Cromwell arrived in Dublin from Milford Haven in August 1649 he was merely the powerful agent of an English society that hated and feared Irish Catholics, represented by 12,000 very battle-hardened soldiers of the New Model Army who would have had nothing but malice in their hearts for the 'papist rebels'. The New Model Army soldiers who made the rough crossing had been selected by ballot – and it was the losers that were on the ships.

The alliance of Royalists and Catholics that had formed in Ireland looked like a formidable and hateful enemy to these soldiers, but in reality it was the English who held all the cards. Leveller influence and power had been checked by the summer of 1649. Now Cromwell could concentrate his fire – literally – on the Irish.

It's clear why Cromwell is remembered as 'God's Englishman' rather than a 'Great Briton'. The other nations of the Isles were seen as enemies, to be defeated and united with England by uncompromising violence. Ireland was always the back door to invade England – and the door was to be bolted shut, no matter what effusion of blood ensued. Ireland was to be secured quickly, preferably with a small number of set-piece battles, and then the Royalists in Scotland would have to be tackled.

Dublin had been secured before Cromwell's arrival and so it was the town of Drogheda which would need to be taken next. Drogheda's name derives from the Irish 'Droichead Átha', meaning 'bridge of the ford', and today it is still an inland port. The River Boyne, which runs through the town, passes into the Irish Sea and allows for the shortest possible sea journey to Britain. Today, Drogheda earns part of its living as a convenient port for all points east, but in 1649 it was Cromwell's first victim, as it allowed an easy sea passage for enemy soldiers and was vital to protect the main road from Dublin to the north.

The town had, and still has, medieval walls up to 20ft high and on average 5ft thick, defensive gates and a stronghold on the top of a Norman motte (or mound). This sounds more impressive than it was. These defences were hundreds of years old even in 1649. The walls and towers, like those of any other trading town, were designed to regulate commerce, and to tax and control goods and people, rather than provide defence against a determined attack.

The defenders still had some reason to hope. These features had been used in a successful defence of the town nine years earlier – the walls had withstood a siege by the Irish rebel leader Phelim O'Neill during the Irish Catholic rebellion of 1641. This event cost the lives of thousands of protestant settlers, if not the number suggested by their propaganda, and the New Model Army and their leader were here for revenge. At the end of the campaign, Cromwell defended the actions of his men in vengeful terms: 'the rebels were made with their blood to answer for the cruelties they had exercised upon diverse poor Protestants'.

O'Neill had wanted to take the town for the same reason as Cromwell, but employed less sophisticated means. He had tried to push through dilapidated parts of the wall or simply climb over using scaling ladders. Cromwell had at his disposal the siege artillery pieces brought over by water for the purpose of destroying walls. It took the Irish 'rebels' four months to fail to take the town in 1641, while the new Model Army did it over the 10/11 of September with no more than 150 deaths. In a relatively short period of time, it had ceased to be the age of the impregnable castle or town.

The only defence that could not be broken was its English, Catholic governor, Sir Arthur Aston. Cromwell knew that the defending forces in Drogheda were never going to surrender; both because he knew the man in charge, and he knew that the defenders understood Drogheda's vital strategic importance. An impasse was inevitable; but at this stage Cromwell kept to the conventions of warfare. On 10 September, Cromwell ordered Aston to surrender the town intact, but both men knew that they were merely going through the motions. Aston was famous and infamous;

he had held Reading against the Parliamentary army in 1643 and now refused to surrender against both overwhelming odds and the 48-pound guns that were outside Drogheda. The Parliament victory at Reading had been messy and bloodthirsty; Drogheda had the added racial element. Cromwell's letter finished with a threat: 'If this is refused, you will have no cause to blame me.'

Cromwell called for the garrison to surrender, and when they didn't, hundreds of cannonballs were used to smash a breach in the wall. Two breaches in the wall were made later in the afternoon of 11 September, 1649. Despite the overwhelming odds in favour of Cromwell, this was the most difficult part of the assault. The holes in the wall would have been blocked with jagged mounds of masonry and this allowed the defenders a last attempt at defence. About 150 of the New Model Army were killed at this point, as their first two attacks were successfully driven off at the Duleek Gate.

By convention, soldiers that did not surrender at the first breach of the wall were not entitled to mercy. Cromwell then issued the order for 'no quarter', which was really not necessary as the conventions of war had already been broken. In any case, their ire was now up; all of the soldiers who successfully entered Drogheda would have had to climb over heaps of corpses from their own side. Cromwell, for the first time since Naseby, took an active front-line role in the fighting.

'No Quarter' was well known and expected; the massacre of civilians was not. It shocked contemporaries in an era that was inured to violence. When rebel soldiers and others hid in St Peter's, Cromwell ordered the burning of the steeple which set the church alight. It never recovered from the attack by the Puritans – it gradually became a ruin and was completely rebuilt in the middle of the eighteenth century. The medieval font is one of the few items that would have been in the church when Cromwell's soldiers set light to it.

Sir Arthur Aston had boasted that anybody who could take Drogheda could take hell; in one way he was obviously wrong but in a horrible sense, his prediction was correct – there was a lot of fire and death on that day. Soldiers fell from the steeple crying: 'My God damn me, I burn!' Officers were bludgeoned to death, priests were murdered, and so were women and children. Soldiers and civilians would be hard to tell apart; some of the New Model would not be worried too much about the distinction. Some of the more horrible stories – children being used as human shields were later dismissed as anti-Cromwellian propaganda. But there were still atrocities.

St Peter's is now part of the Church of Ireland – a protestant body with members in Northern Ireland and the Republic. There is another, Catholic, St Peter's Church South of the Boyne, which is a late nineteenth-century church in the gothic style. The head of Oliver Plunkett rests there, a Catholic martyr who opposed the Cromwellian settlement in Ireland and was later accused of treason and executed at Tyburn in 1681, in the same place as Cromwell had been re-executed twenty years earlier. Plunkett's head was installed in St Peter's Catholic Church in 1921, in an act that Cromwell and people like him would have viewed as abhorrent and superstitious.

One surviving defensive landmark is Millmount, originally a Norman motte and bailey castle and part of the town walls in 1649. Its distinctive shape can be seen from all parts of the town; the locals call it the 'Cup and Saucer'. This is where Sir Arthur Aston and many of the rebel forces retired, and where many were killed. A number of them were English, but were murdered none the less. Aston himself was beaten to death with his wooden leg, wrenched from him in the false belief that it was full of gold.

The behaviour of the New Model Army, and the tacit agreement of Cromwell, is shocking to people today. They certainly shocked some people at the time, but Cromwell was not one of them. Cromwell had behaved the same in England, famously at the siege of Basing House, Hampshire, in October 1645. In 1649, he was more than happy to put the details in writing. He reported back to Parliament that 2,000 soldiers and many civilians had been killed.

Cromwell was part of a movement of people with the same beliefs – it was John Pickering at Basing House and John Hewson and Daniel Axtell at Drogheda, ready to behave in the same way as Cromwell with the same justification that seems abhorrent to us today. Both Hewson and Axtell wanted this army to be put to the sword rather than allow them to fight again; if, in the confusion, some civilians died, then that was no matter.

The Millmount Museum, near the tower, can be visited and offers either a guided or independent tour of the history of Drogheda over three floors. The museum also allows the visitor to walk to the top of the tower which gives an impressive view of the town. The 360 degree view is the reason for the strategic importance of the fortification in the first place; and the original hill would have been even higher, as its size was partly reduced in the 1840s.

The tower and fortifications were rebuilt in 1810, and remained more-or-less intact until the Irish civil war in 1922 – another reminder of the suffering of Ireland caused by centuries of British intervention. Much of the wall is still visible in the town to this day, as the aim of Cromwell's soldiers was to breach the wall in one place, invade the town, and as it turned out, kill many of the inhabitants. The absence of wall in most parts of Drogheda is due to later developments.

St Laurence's Gate, a fine example of a thirteenth-century barbican, is further example of how old Drogheda is. It is one of the best examples of its kind in the UK and Ireland, and last saw action in the Irish rebellion of 1641; the New Model Army entered the town at another part of the wall. The gate, a structure designed to control traffic and trade, was nearly destroyed by modern juggernauts getting stuck and other vehicles damaging it. It is now traffic-free, and you can safely go round the back to get an idea of what the walls would have looked like.

If the later history of the town is of interest, then a visit to the Battle of the Boyne Visitor Centre would complement a day in Drogheda – it is fifteen minutes by car, with public transport also available. It tells the story of the battle of 1690, arguably the last battle of a civil war between Charles's younger son, James II, and the preferred Protestant alternative for Parliament, William of Orange.

Two towns come to mind as being victims of Cromwell's fanatical New Model Army – Drogheda and Wexford, but the whole of Ireland suffered from Cromwell's actions. The later history of Ireland was blighted by the way that conquest and colonisation became the norm, and extreme violence seen as the answer to what only the British called the 'Irish problem'. The attack on Wexford is often forgotten by the English; less so by the Irish. Cromwell decided to strike Wexford 'while the fear of God is upon them'. He meant this literally; it was God that was creating these victories over the Irish, and he was just the agent. The geographical imperative was the same as Drogheda. Wexford was a convenient and safe port both for the English, their political enemies, and pirates. The town is situated on the south side of the mouth of the River Slaney, with its harbour protected by a peninsula of land on both sides and by Fort Rosslare. Fort Rosslare

Astrological Chart. (*Wellcome Collection, London*)

The execution warrant, 1649.

War as teamwork, 1644. A long-haired Cromwell is second left.

One man's triumph, or is it God's? Dunbar 1651.

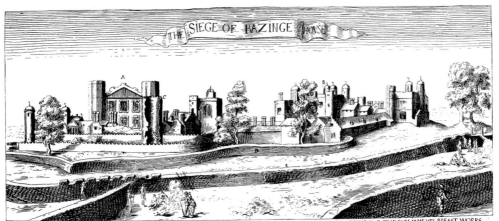

THE SIEGE OF BAZINGE HOVSE

A. THE OLDE HOVSE . B. THE NEW. C. THE TOWER THAT IS HALFE BATTERED DOWNE . D. THE KINGES BREAST WORKS . E. THE PARLIAMENTS BREAST WORKS .

HOLLAR'S VIEW OF BASING HOUSE c. 1644

Basing House, the year before Cromwell arrived.

The Siege of Basing House, 1645.

Dignified equestrian portrait of a ruler Charles I.

OLIVERIVS CROMWELL.

An attempt to create legitimacy using the same image.

Oliver Cromwell, Lord Protector.
(*Wellcome Collection, London*)

Cromwell at Drogheda,
1649. In reality, he fought
his way in.

In league with the devil.

Unnatural, comic usurper.

The LORD PROTECTOR lying in State at Sommerset House.

Engraved by J.ᵉˢ Caldwall, from the original print in the Collection of JOHN TOWNELEY ESQ.ᴿ

The 'King' is dead, 1658. (*Wellcome Collection, London*)

1. *Cromwels haupt.*   2. *Bratſhew.*   3. *Ireton*

Cromwell's post-mortem execution, 1661.

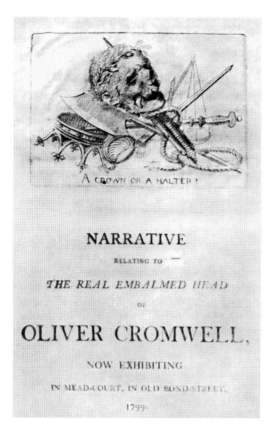

Curious exhibit, 1799.

Head of state.

survived the civil war but was abandoned to the sea in the 1920s – at a low tide some of the ruins can be seen in the harbour.

The fort had to be taken before the ships carrying the siege engines could disembark. It was attacked by the Parliamentary navy under Henry Ireton, and the fort itself was stormed with some cruelty to civilians by Michael Jones, the commander who had secured Dublin before Cromwell arrived. Jones's army rounded up the wives and children left behind and forced them to trudge along to the cavern (long since disappeared) facing the spot where the post office now stands. Despite their pleas and the heart-rending shrieks, they were all massacred without mercy. Michael Jones has not been forgotten in Wexford, although the place of his massacres is still called 'Cromwell's Murder Hole'. It is a reminder that both blame and credit for the cruel success of the English Parliamentary forces in Ireland needs to be distributed more equitably. Without this bloody teamwork, Cromwell would not have been able to install six siege pieces on Wexford Rocks.

On 3 October, Cromwell made the same formulaic demand for surrender, common to any siege on the British mainland. He had the confident tone of a man whose siege artillery had followed him by sea and whose plan seemed to be succeeding. Trim and Dundalk had surrendered without a fight, but this would not happen at Wexford. The governor, Colonel David Synott, refused an immediate surrender and played for time. Refusing the first demand was a standard part of the 'siege script'; indeed any less would have earned him a court martial. Synott's demands were excessive and Cromwell was within his rights to reject them. Then the gates were opened for the English by a turncoat called James Stafford. When the New Model Army entered, the amateur defenders panicked and were killed in their thousands. The Bullring in the centre of town was the site of the worst events.

Civilians bearing arms were killed. Hundreds of soldiers and others were drowned trying to escape by boat. These atrocities were not ordered by Cromwell, but he approved of them. It was 'the righteous judgement of God'. Unlike in Drogheda, however, Cromwell does not especially mention mass civilian deaths in his report to Parliament, although it seems certain that there were at least the same number as at Drogheda. His only regret was that all the houses were destroyed, and there was nowhere for his army of saints to shelter in the winter. Cromwell had lost around twenty men; the defenders nearer 2,000.

Two thirds of Wexford's walls still exist in some form. All but one of the gates has disappeared, the victim of later traffic management, as in many similar expanding towns from the late eighteenth century onwards. Westgate is the only surviving entrance to the town but it was never a main entrance, and that probably explains its survival; it was a private entrance for the clergy which allowed them to avoid paying taxes. Wexford and the other towns taken by Oliver Cromwell were ancient before he arrived and survived his deprecations. They survive to this day as part of an independent, increasingly secular Ireland largely free from British influence and control. What would Cromwell have made of that?

Chapter Fourteen

'Sorrows Ended'
Worcester 1651

Worcester, like Oxford, Newark, Drogheda or Colchester, has a proud civil war history of supporting the king until the very end. Like Marston Moor, Naseby, Preston and Dunbar, it was also one of the places where the Royalist dream was snuffed out by Oliver Cromwell. It was the beginning and end of the civil war; the first skirmish was in the town, at Powick Bridge, on 23 September 1642 and the last battle was in Worcester itself on 3 September 1651, when the Royalist army was eliminated. Worcester's reputation as the last act of the civil war is most famously expressed by Cromwell's Puritan preacher friend Hugh Peters, who bade farewell to the militia after the battle with an echo of the famous 'Henry V' speech:

> when their wives and children should ask them where they had been and what news, they should say they had been at Worcester, where England's sorrows began, and where they were happily ended.

Worcester was a Royalist town for all of the war from 15 November 1642 until its surrender on the king's orders in July 1646. It was occupied by the Parliamentarian army for a month until 19 October 1642. One of the occupying soldiers was Nehemiah Wharton, a London apprentice very much of the Puritan persuasion. Wharton was an enthusiastic volunteer for Parliament whose letters back home suggested that he pillaged and plundered, yet at the same time destroyed the popish decorations he saw on the way. He was, literally, damning about Worcester: 'so papistical, atheistical and abominable that it resembles Sodom and is the very emblem of Gomorrah'. He was a man thinking for himself and translating his thoughts into action in a way that only war can make possible.

Nehemiah entered Worcester on 26 September 1642 with his regiment, who proceeded to destroy the 'popish' cathedral organ, burn prayer books and smash windows and decorations in a building that had recently been beautified on the instructions of Laud and Charles. Men like Wharton were seen riding round town in remnants of 'popish' surplices. Despite this, his letters home showed that he enjoyed his tourist visit to the cathedral – this would not have stopped him purging it of 'popery'.

As an independent religious thinker and enthusiast for total war, Nehemiah was ahead of his time, and would never have heard the name of Oliver Cromwell at this early stage. He was – metaphorically and literally – a mere foot soldier under the control of the Earl of Essex, 'Old Robin'. It was Essex who condoned the cleansing/destruction of the cathedral, not Cromwell. Essex is often seen as the moderate to Cromwell's extremist, but it was Essex who first gutted religious buildings, killed Irish catholic prisoners of war as a matter of course, and who suffered (but did not encourage) men like Wharton in his army – as long as they had no voice. While Worcester Cathedral was under attack, the Parliament in London were destroying the organ at the old St Paul's Cathedral and arresting those who protested. None of this was due to Cromwell.

Here, in one man, was a prediction of the way that the war would proceed. It was Cromwell who first built up an army of Nehemiah Whartons – with perhaps a little more discipline than the man himself showed – an army that destroyed the Anglican church and executed the king. This did not include Nehemiah personally as his letters stop around the time of the Battle of Edgehill. He may have died there or at the later Royalist victory at Brentford. But it was men like Wharton that made an Oliver Cromwell figure possible; to use an analogy that would have meant nothing to them, in terms of the changes caused by the civil war, Cromwell was the surfboard and not the wave.

Worcester was a thorn in the side of the Parliamentarians but it played little part in Cromwell's furious riding up and down the country; although Cromwell's military activity in the south of England did greatly inconvenience the town during the war. It became important again in the later summer of 1651; but the revolution that had taken place in the meantime meant that the outcome would be different from that in 1642.

In late August 1651, Charles II found himself occupying Worcester and organising a last stand against the New Model Army and the militia. Cromwell had engineered this difficult position for the king. After the defeat at Dunbar in 1650, it was Cromwell who had encouraged Charles to break out of Scotland with a Scottish Presbyterian army, which looked a lot like a foreign invading power to people in England. This is one of the reasons the North of England did not rise for the new king, and why Charles II found himself isolated in the south west.

Cromwell rode furiously through the Midlands, supported by a battle-hardened New Model Army, local militias flocking to oppose the Scots, and thousands of others who could clearly see the winning side and wished to be on it. For all the unpopularity of the Rump and men like Cromwell, Cromwell's military and political manoeuvrings had made Charles desperate and on the run.

What was going through Cromwell's mind as he went through the Midlands? There would be anger that the Scots were going against the will of the Almighty, supporting a cause that the Lord himself had condemned through His signs. There was also practicality – Cromwell ordered thousands of pickaxes and shovels in case he needed to besiege the town. As it turned out, Charles II opted for battle and the tools were not necessary; Cromwell was trusting in God, but also making practical provisions, as was always his way.

Worcester still has its civil war monuments, such as Fort Royal Park, a place where Cromwell would have been physically present. This was, and still is, the highest point in Worcester, and earlier in the war the Parliamentary army had used its strategic location to bomb the city over the Severn. Charles II had placed his artillery there and its capture was Cromwell's first aim. It was overrun after heavy fighting; the guns were turned inwards on the Scots, who fled into the centre of town and smashed into their allies being pushed by Colonel Fleetwood's soldiers in the west. Cromwell was no armchair general. He led from the front at Worcester – loudly offering quarter to the Scots (these were Presbyterians, not Catholics; but they still gave their answer by trying to shoot him). Cromwell's entry into the town turned the tide against the Royalists and, as ever, he received the plaudits, but just like most of Cromwell's battles, he had superior resources and excellent support from others.

The hill is peaceful now, and not as high as it was in the seventeenth century, as it was slighted and the star-shaped fortification destroyed by Cromwell after his victory. It would have been carnage on 3 September and it would have been witnessed by Charles II himself, who was stationed at the top of the Cathedral Tower watching his Scottish allies being squashed into central Worcester and their corpses blocking up the medieval streets. Later in the battle, Charles led a desperate charge against Colonel Fleetwood before escaping the field.

It was all very, very one sided. The tired Royalist army had 13,000, Parliament had twice that figure with endless scope for reinforcements. Only 200 of Cromwell's men were killed whilst the cathedral was overflowing with Scottish and Royalist prisoners.

Today, information boards are provided by the Battle of Worcester Society and part of the battlefield at Powick Bridge is still accessible by footpath. The Society holds regular commemorations on 3 September.

In front of Fort Royal Park is the Commandery. William, Duke of Hamilton was a general in the army of Charles II and made the building his headquarters before the battle. Hamilton was wounded in the leg, and was carried back to the Commandery and laid in what is now called the 'Death and Loss' room, where he died. Like many war wounds, it was infection and not the original injury that killed Hamilton. His body was buried under the floor, and only later was it transferred to the cathedral.

The Commandery may have been the headquarters of the Royalists but it is now a major attraction for all aspects of the civil war. The fact that it was opened as late as 1977, and was Britain's only museum dedicated to the civil war until the opening of the National Civil War Museum in Newark in 2015, tells you a lot about our attitude to the events. These days it deals with all of Worcester's history, as the Tudor building and grounds have a history beyond these years and the museum authorities want to emphasise this era as well; but the civil war is to the forefront.

As ever with museums that want to attract young people, there are dressing-up activities and a themed play area on Fort Royal Park. Like most British museums, the Commandery tries to engage its visitors in a modern way. There is an interactive experience – Worcester's Civil War Story – 'taking you back 350 years into a murky, conflicted 17th century Worcester of fiery debates, gunpowder and dank city streets'. You can also interact with Cromwell himself – in a war of words rather than an actual war. After Cromwell's death, a wax mould was made of his face which was used to make several plaster death masks and the museum has one of these on display.

Worcester's motto – 'Civitas in Bello et Pace Fidelis' – 'The City faithful in war and in peace', is still on the town's crest today. Worcester remains proud of its anti-Cromwellian sentiments, and continued to exploit its reputation as 'The Faithful City' long after the Restoration. About five minutes walk from the Commandery is the Worcester Guildhall, featuring statues of the two Charles on each side of the main door with what is reputed to be Oliver Cromwell's head pinned to the wall over the main entrance. The head was added in the nineteenth century by a populace that had neither forgiven nor forgotten. Some historians have suggested that the tortured face is merely a copy of statues put outside courts of law in medieval times to remind people of the pain inflicted on those who challenge the establishment. Either way, the victory for the ruling class is made obvious.

The Battle of Worcester was the end of the civil war; this was largely understood at the time and the date is sometimes seen as significant. The Battles of Dunbar, Worcester and the Protector's death all happened on 3 September. This would have been seen by some to be a sign, and there is some circumstantial evidence that Cromwell was aware of it. On 29 August, he took time to march to Upton-on-Severn to congratulate Lambert's troops who had secured the bridge over the river. A plaque in the town records Cromwell's reception on that day in 1651: Oliver Cromwell was greeted here 'with abundance of joy and extraordinary shouting'. It was clear that everything was in place for the battle on 2 September and Cromwell seemed to have been stringing out events a little, which was his *modus operandi* in civilian matters, while on the battlefield he was better known for apparent recklessness.

The modern mind might think that his deliberate prevarication, to reach the appointed date, meant that it 'didn't count'. That's not the way Cromwell would have seen it. The watchword for the day was 'The Lord of Hosts', the same as the battle of Dunbar exactly a year earlier, and in his first letter back to the Commons, Cromwell was still aware: 'upon this day … remarkable for a mercy vouchsafed to your forces on this twelvemonth in Scotland'. On the way back from Worcester, his chaplain Hugh Peters noted that Cromwell was particularly elevated in his mood – a possible euphemism for the emotional outbursts he was prone to. Lucy Hutchinson, a Puritan enemy of Cromwell, believed this was the point where his belief that he was the instrument of the Almighty reached a hubristic peak.

On his deathbed on Monday 2 September, seven years later, he was apparently ready to depart this life. He rambled and was irascible, but his main concern was his favour in the eyes of the Lord. He then rallied, but died in the afternoon of Tuesday 3 September. He was impatient to the end; when offered a drink on his deathbed he replied: 'It is not my design to drink or to sleep, but my design is to make what haste I can to be gone'. Was he holding on for the date? Did he even know what day of the week it was?

Chapter Fifteen

Fit for a King?
Whitehall
Hampton Court Palace
1654–1658

It becomes harder to follow Cromwell's footsteps after the Battle of Worcester. Cromwell's career then entered its purely political phase, which was to turn out to be less successful, but far more comfortable than his military one. His comprehensive victory meant that he no longer needed to be geographically mobile. After 1651 there was no more widespread Royalist resistance, and Cromwell became a London-based politician until his death in 1658. His furious riding stops after 1652; there is one recorded visit to Dover and Deal. The rest of the time he is in central London, or supervising the building and launching of ships in Woolwich. As Lord Protector, he had acquired substantial property in Buckinghamshire and Essex, but there is no firm evidence that he ever visited them. Whatever the reasons for taking on the government of the nation, it was not from personal greed, and perhaps significantly, avarice was never high up on the Royalist's stream of accusations. Ambition, though, was a different matter.

As Cromwell rose politically, so did the status of the buildings in which he lived. In recognition of his new position as one of the most powerful men in Britain, he moved his whole family to Holborn in about 1646. At the time it was a new suburb of London with large open spaces and market gardens. He had another base in London after February 1650, when the Rump Parliament gave him an official residence at the Cockpit in Whitehall, formerly the London home of the Earl of Pembroke. It was given to him in his capacity as the Lord Lieutenant of Ireland. The whole of the Whitehall complex was destroyed in a fire in 1698, but you can get a sense of the politically central location of the Cockpit by the fact that the Earl of Pembroke was able to watch the execution of the king from a bedroom window. Cromwell himself could not have been far away on that fateful day.

In December 1653, Cromwell was invested as Lord Protector of the Commonwealth at Westminster Hall. It is here that he became a king in all but name until his death on 3 September 1658. He ruled England, Scotland and Ireland under a succession of plans and constitutions, devised principally by his supporters in the army. The invented title of 'Lord Protector' failed to disguise the fact that he possessed more power than any other ruler in British history. He was called 'Your Highness' and was genuinely feared and respected by major foreign powers. He lived in splendour in Hampton Court Palace and the Palace of Whitehall.

Cromwell's reason for choosing Hampton Court is not really known; he may have had no choice. The Rump Parliament sold most of the Royal assets after 1649 with the belief that no one person would be needed to help them rule the new commonwealth. In a move that rather showed the real nature of the new regime, the Rump had decided that Windsor, Somerset House and the Tower of London would be reserved for the army. Richmond Palace was to be sold off, so there was not much choice for Cromwell.

The Rump could not make its mind up about Hampton Court Palace. It sold off and re-purchased part of the property between 1649 and 1653. The palace then had to be filled up with new art and furniture. The issue became more urgent when it became clear that the Rump's failure to govern either with efficiency or popularity meant that rule by a single person was politically necessary. When Cromwell lost patience with the Rump and dissolved it by force in April 1653, his comment, 'You have sat too long here for any good you have been doing', applied to its administration of the country's assets as well as everything else it tried to do.

Whitehall Palace may have been lost but Hampton Court still stands in judgement on Cromwell's real motives and ambitions. Hampton Court Palace is evidence for the prosecution as far as his enemies are concerned. Cromwell's new accommodation in palaces was, to some, a bricks-and-mortar expression of his hypocrisy and ambition and the unnaturalness of the state of affairs.

Cromwell's critics assert that his removal of the Rump Parliament, his investiture in Westminster Hall and his installation into his two palaces are all causally connected. It was all part of a plan going back to 1649, or even 1642. In any case, by April 1654 Cromwell and his family were living in the main part of Whitehall Palace and political business was enacted there during the week. His wife and his mother lived there too and would have preferred something more modest, but the Cockpit was no place to greet the ambassadors of France and Spain and impress them suitably. The republican government needed to survive by creating palaces fit for a king.

The Lord Protector also needed an out of town residence. The stripped-down republican government, who had deluded themselves that they would never need an individual leader in a palace, had only Hampton Court to offer. It was not all bad news – it was still a luxurious place, far enough from London to be a place of weekend relaxation, and like all former royal palaces, it was on a river route to London for easy access.

Cromwell knew the building well. He had arranged for it to be a place of detention for the king and it is there that unsuccessful peace negotiations had taken place in 1647. Five years earlier, the king had chosen it as a place of escape after the uproar caused by his attempted assault on the five members in January 1642. It was convenient as a prison and a refuge for one reason only – it was just the right distance from London. Securing your prisoner was far from easy though. It was a 1000-room building that was impossible to defend without a troop of horse. Cromwell's ally, Edmund Waller, was in charge of that troop and feared, correctly as it turned out, that escape would be quite easy. It was better as a court, and because of the lenient way that Charles was treated in 1647 it still looked a bit like one, with Charles allowed to move quite freely, have attendants and hold receptions.

If Charles had been in a proper prison, he may not have been able to get away; it was by escaping from Hampton Court in November 1647 that he broke his parole and guaranteed a second civil war. It would have been around this time that Cromwell decided that Charles's tenure on the throne was no longer viable. Sometime in 1648, probably quite late, Cromwell was converted to removing the king. According to his enemies, Hampton Court Palace was one of the rewards for his perfidy.

Cromwell's court at Whitehall would have been recognisable to any Royalist. The key question about the monarchical-looking arrangements was Cromwell's attitude to it. To those sympathetic to him, he was trying to create a court that reflected a strong, stable and legitimate government with an established head of state. To others, Cromwell loved the new court without the need to justify its existence. This was the view of both Royalists and republicans, who thought it was unnatural and insulting to the monarchy. For the Royalists, Cromwell was not the legitimate monarch, and for the republicans, nobody was.

Most Friday evenings the court would decamp to East Moseley by road or barge under conditions of great security. Cromwell the great traverser of the three kingdoms had become a mere commuter. He may have had a court, but unlike those of the Tudor and Stuart monarchy, he could not rely on the deference of the country gentry and aristocracy to give him a bed for the night. He stayed in London.

Cromwell wanted art and decoration to give credibility to his court. Some of the masterpieces on display today were bought by Charles I but saved from being sold by Cromwell. Whitehall Palace still had an art gallery in the 1650s, though greatly depleted. Cromwell was very happy to have pagan, classical and pre-reformation art on display there. Had some of these latter images appeared in a church, they would have been destroyed by Puritans, with Cromwell's approval and support.

Charles's own suite and bedroom on the upper floor was emptied of furniture and unoccupied while Cromwell was there. This was more a result of the Rump's fire sale of the king's possessions than any concern about replacing the king in his bedroom. Instead, Cromwell used Queen Henrietta Maria's apartment on the more favoured east side of the palace. Only break with precedent was that Cromwell and his wife Elizabeth slept together regularly in the same bedroom.

Some of the tapestries and paintings were put there by Henry VIII. In the Long Gallery, where Cromwell would greet foreign ambassadors, there was Andrea Mantegna's series of late fifteenth-century renaissance masterpieces *The Triumph of Caesar*, purchased by Charles I in 1629. They were put up for sale by the Rump and had already been valued at a remarkable £5,019, but Cromwell wished to keep them. Caesar is shown defeating his foreign enemies by military conquest, followed by a Roman triumph. It is a solemn celebration of a military rather than a political leader, and war is not glamourized for its own sake. There is no mention of assassination and civil war, and its classical origin guaranteed that no Catholic victories would be celebrated. It's clear why Cromwell liked it. They are still available to be seen in Hampton Court – in a display case to protect them from the environment.

The Chapel Royal was already an important part of British history before the civil war. It was the place where Archbishop Cranmer handed over documents to Henry VIII detailing the adulteries of Henry's fifth wife Katherine Howard in 1540. Three years earlier, newly finished and perhaps the last Catholic chapel built in England, it had been the place where Henry's son Edward was baptised. Edward VI was a thoroughgoing Protestant whose reign as king was cut short by his premature death in 1553. If Edward had survived, there may have been no Catholic Queen Mary, no 'virgin' Queen Elizabeth, no need for a messy religious compromise and no Stuart monarchy which helped provoke civil war – and therefore no famous Oliver Cromwell.

The magnificent chapel suffered during the war, but at the hands of the Puritans of 1641 rather than the Lord Protector of 1656. When the king was imprisoned there in 1647, it was the zealots of the army who destroyed the decorations on the walls. The mood must have been ugly; even non-religious symbols on the seats and stalls were destroyed. The Tudor ceiling was too high for the soldiers to strip off the carvings and Cromwell would have recognised the Tudor Roses as similar to his grandfather's loyal ceiling symbols at Hinchingbrooke.

Cromwell's court was an ordered, decorous affair that was designed to add dignity to the new regime. It was a place where bad behaviour was discouraged and in that regard it was similar to that of Charles I. The only difference was that Cromwell's own behaviour was often silly and childish, and it does seem that when this happened, people in court were meant to applaud his behaviour and find it amusing. He was prone to abuse his position a little – for example, having a gong sounded in the middle of dinner and having people's unfinished food snatched from them by soldiers. He was also known to tease people about their links to the Stuarts. He had shown this 'childish' sense of humour on previous occasions. Before the battle of Dunbar in 1650, he was helpless with laughter when his soldiers opened barrels of cream and smeared themselves with it.

There were two 'royal' weddings in 1657. When his daughter Mary was married in November, he crushed his daughter's headdress, daubed sticky sweetmeats on chairs before people could sit on them, and sprayed the ladies' dresses with a sweet and sickly dessert wine. His enemies suggested that this was not the behaviour of a monarch. Cromwell also flicked ink around when collecting signatures for the execution of the king. He once threw pillows at fellow regicide Edmund Ludlow and ran away. His messing about was probably nothing to do with his new exalted position – it was always in his personality to have such a childlike sense of humour.

There were other contradictions more serious than a dodgy sense of humour. Both of Cromwell's daughters were openly called princesses. Frances was married to Robert Rich, the grandson of Cromwell's former political patron the Earl of Warwick. There was mixed dancing at the celebration; hardly the mark of a Puritan. Oliver Cromwell allowed his other daughter Mary to be married in the Chapel Royal to Viscount Falconbridge on 17 November 1657, using the traditional Anglican marriage rite, although the use of the Book of Common Prayer was against the law during the Commonwealth.

Organ music and opera were allowed in the Protector's court and Cromwell had the organ taken from Oxford University for his own use. In fairness, Puritans only objected to music in a religious context and opera was meant to be uplifting, but this sounded pretentious and snobby to some. In 1656, while Cromwell's major generals were suppressing wrestling around the country, Cromwell was watching it in the (recently sold) Hyde Park. Cromwell was accused of snobbery by his Victorian critics for housing his officers within the palace grounds but relegating the ordinary soldiers to a public house, the Toy Inn. There is a plaque near the maze that marks its location. However, there is another way of looking at this; Cromwell had the inn built especially. Most soldiers in the civil war were used to sleeping tentless, outdoors.

Cromwell persisted with art that would not have pleased his religious friends. The bronze Diana statue commissioned by Charles I for his wife was moved to the Privy Garden from Somerset House on the order of the Lord Protector in 1656. Diana, the classical goddess of hunting, is shown full size, lightly dressed, in a short tunic tied above the waist and looped over her shoulder leaving one breast bare. The statue is a five minute walk from the maze, in the round pond at Bushey Park. It is worth seeing to challenge the established view of Cromwell's Puritanism. Some people, with perhaps less historical perspective, have voiced concern that it is a poor likeness of Lady Diana Spencer.

Was there meant to be a new Cromwell dynasty at Hampton Court? The provisional answer has to be in the affirmative from the evidence we have. In 2001 a plan of Hampton Court in the time of Cromwell was discovered in the papers of George Legge, the first Baron Dartmouth. The plan, now in the archives at Kew, dates from 1656 and clearly shows the Cromwell family monogram on the newly installed drainpipe heads.

It was never quite clear who was to succeed Cromwell when he died. Some assumed that it would be a member of the army council; others that it would be one of the sons of the Protector. In 1657 he was given the right to name his own successor under yet another written constitution, the Humble Petition and Advice. Cromwell was granted power that Charles could have only dreamt about, but without the name of king. Throughout his life Cromwell made no clear comment on the succession, but eventually his eldest son Richard Cromwell (born 1626) became the new Protector. Cromwell's younger son, Henry Cromwell (born 1628) was a much more astute and able politician, and a man who was prepared to serve in Ireland while Richard had to be dragged from a life of hunting and shooting with the gentry in Hampshire. Henry would have been a better choice. Oliver's hagiographer Thomas Carlyle, thought so. Henry was,

> A brave man and true ... had he been named Protector there had most likely been quite another History of England to write.

It was never an option however, and not just because Henry was opposed to it. The hereditary principle prevailed, which produced a mediocre replacement for Oliver Cromwell in the same way as it had done in the case of James I.

Perhaps mediocre is the wrong word to describe Oliver's successor – Richard 'Tumbledown Dick' Cromwell. He did not inherit his father's reputation, his support system in the army or his father's desire to work hard. He did inherit Cromwell's lack of legitimacy and his father's failure to create a political system greater than the willpower of one special man. He did inherit Hampton Court, and one of Richard's lesser problems was the threat that it would be sold again to repay debts.

By 1660, Richard was gone, being unable to control either the army or Parliament in the way that Cromwell did. The real reason for failure was the inability to build a government by consent, so a monarchy became the only alternative. The next occupant of Hampton Court was General Monck, another man whose clever use of an army gained him a palace. Monck and his army had crucially changed sides and allowed a bloodless end to the Cromwell regime and was rewarded by the occupation of the palace for his lifetime, which was really no more or no less than Cromwell achieved himself.

Part Four

A BODY

Chapter Sixteen

Cromwell the Corpse 1658–1661
Westminster Abbey
Tyburn

Oliver Cromwell was last seen on a cold winter's morning in January 1661. His face was turned towards Whitehall, in the direction of the Banqueting House, where exactly twelve years earlier Charles I had been executed. We do not need to anticipate his thoughts – he had none; he was dead. He had been dug up, 'executed', and his body dismembered.

When your enemies feel the need to dig up and desecrate your corpse, your position in history is assured. It is a back-handed compliment to 'execute' somebody that is already dead, and then obliterate their remains. Alongside Cromwell and the regicides we can add early Protestant John Wycliffe, Rasputin, and another challenger to the English monarchy, Simon De Montfort. De Montfort was mutilated after the Battle of Evesham in 1265 in the heat of conflict; Cromwell, a more successful usurper who had died in power rather than in defeat, was revenged with much colder calculation.

Cromwell had spent his first twenty-seven months of death in Westminster Abbey in a magnificent tomb that befitted a man who was the unchallengeable ruler of Britain. When Cromwell died in 1658, he was embalmed and laid in state like other rulers before him. In the same vault were his mother, sister and son-in-law; all of these people had predeceased him, which was to turn out to be an inconvenience for all concerned when it came to taking them all out again.

When the monarchy was restored in 1660, the son of the executed king wanted revenge on the regicides, and the fact that Cromwell was dead did not make any difference. Joining Cromwell on the list for post-mortem execution were Henry Ireton, John Bradshaw, the judge who condemned Charles to death, and Thomas Pride, who purged Parliament of the king's supporters in 1648. Pride was soon dropped because his place of burial was hard to discover in the short time they had.

After exhumation, for which the monarchy paid a local mason John Lewis fifteen shillings (and, uncharacteristically, paid up quite quickly), Cromwell and Ireton spent the night of 29 January lying insensible in the Red Lion Inn, Holborn, perhaps a first for these two Puritans. Bradshaw joined them the next day – the second-rate lawyer from Congleton was not a pleasant house guest. Bradshaw had not had the advantage of being embalmed, and despite being dead a mere fourteen months was reportedly a green, stinking corpse.

The present Red Lion Square is named after the inn and was an unusual place to stash the bodies for a night, as it was not an obvious route from Westminster Abbey to Tyburn. It was nearly twice as long as the direct journey; it seems they were following, as far as they could, the traditional route which would have begun at Newgate – the starting place for traitors. One of many myths about Cromwell's corpse is that it was replaced at the inn with the less decomposed body of a soldier. For a start, Cromwell was not decomposed very much and men who were prepared to double the length of their journey to make a symbolic point were hardly likely to replace the miscreant with an innocent soldier.

The pub has been rebuilt since then; this has not stopped Cromwell's ghost haunting the area. It must be the busiest ghost in British history. This is fair enough. Cromwell rode furiously around Britain for most of the 1640s, so it seems reasonable that his ghost should do the same.

The three corpses were taken to Tyburn, a village to the west of London and tied to a sled in the manner reserved for traitors. Tyburn was a traditional place of execution. There, Cromwell's coffin was propped up and opened. His green cerecloth shroud made him stand out and his kingly embalming made him far less objectionable. A Spanish witness noted that 'Cromwell had been very fresh'. They had been so keen to avoid corruption that he had been simply and privately buried – in Puritan fashion – at a date soon after 10 November, before his funeral on 23 November 1658. On that day, Cromwell's £4,000 hearse was empty – this was common knowledge and not without precedent for other great men.

The three corpses were gibbeted until sunset on the Tyburn Tree, a triangular scaffold that could execute three people at a time. At the end of the day, all three were roughly decapitated and their bodies thrown into the common pit. Their exact resting place is unknown. It would be approximately in the triangle of Marble Arch, Edgware Road and

Bayswater Road. In 1860, a large number of bones were discovered after building work in what is now Connaught Square. There is also a plaque on a traffic island near the Edgware Road which has recently been enhanced with three young trees – perhaps one for each regicide; or perhaps not.

This was not the way it was meant to be. The original tomb in Westminster Abbey was a magnificent and expensive creation showing Cromwell in full effigy. The tomb was destroyed at the time of the Restoration and now there is only an estimated location. A stone marking the spot was laid on the floor by the liberal theologian Dean Arthur Stanley during the Victorian era, when Cromwell's reputation was recovering. The stone is presently covered up with a carpet in what is now the RAF chapel, then the Henry VII chapel. When the carpet was moved in 2009, it was a news item; perhaps even Cromwell's enemies today may see this small stone as insufficient recognition of a major historical figure. There is also a small modern marker with a stripped-back, factual message.

THE BURIAL PLACE OF OLIVER CROMWELL 1658–1661

In September 1661, after the main culprits had been dealt with, there was a mass clear out of those who were deemed unworthy of being buried with the ruling class, especially the other members of the Cromwell family. The only exception to this was the body of Cromwell's favoured daughter Elizabeth Claypole, who died in August 1658, a month before her father, whose grief was said at the time to have accelerated his own death. She still lies in the Abbey, and a small modern stone marks her place of burial. It seems that the vengeful Royalists missed her.

Not all the civil war leaders were removed from the Abbey; only those who had presumed to replace the ruling class. The Earl of Essex, who died in 1646 and was on the receiving end of lots of criticism for his lukewarm approach to fighting the king, is still in the Abbey, resting in the St John the Baptist chapel. These two facts are certainly related.

It seems that the Cromwell family were removed from the vault to reach some regicides who had been interred beforehand – they might have merely been collateral damage, but some historians have suggested that it was a deliberate attempt to destroy a hated, if unsuccessful, dynastic rival. It was a form of retribution for the hubris of burying Cromwell among the relatives of legitimate monarchs.

A minute's walk away from the Abbey is the church of St Margaret's Westminster, a church linked with British politics since its adoption as the parish church of the House of Commons in 1614. The short distance must have been convenient when moving the putrefying bodies of Cromwell's mother and sister and the nineteen others to be burned and then buried in a pit in the graveyard. Elizabeth Cromwell did not even wish to be in the Abbey – her request for a simple burial was ignored and instead there was a magnificent torch-lit ceremony, 'the needless ceremonies and great expense which the protector put the public to in burying her gave great offence to the republicans', said hostile Royalist historian Mark Noble. It seemed that one thing the republicans and monarchists had in common was the hatred of this new upstart dynasty.

Chapter Seventeen

Cromwell's Changing Reputation
I – The Age of Fear and Hatred 1661–1850

It was the historian E.H. Carr who commented that history was used mostly to solve the problems of the present, and for the 350 years since his death, this has been true about interpretations of Cromwell. After a generation or two had passed and Cromwell had slipped out of living memory, people started to interpret him for their own time and its preoccupations. His continued greatness lies in the fact that people with different views still feel the need to interpret him. His complex personality and actions in life means that there is suitable material for all ideologies to use. The disadvantage is that these qualities create division on matters such as religion and politics that would profit from a consensus.

An overview of Cromwell's reputation would look roughly like this: obloquy for around 100 years until about 1770, then an improvement from the time of the American and French Revolutions until the rise of Napoleon, followed by a long revival (roughly 1850 to 1920) and then decline until the 1950s, then a rise, and it could be argued, a general decline in more recent years.

Cromwell was unpopular with most people in Britain when he died in 1658, except for the new ruling elite. The stormy weather around the time of his death was interpreted by many as the devil taking him away. Monarchists were relieved, but then became disappointed when there was no Royalist rising. They overestimated their own popularity; the Cromwellian system had to destroy itself before the monarchy could be restored. This had been a government of a hard, determined man and his army. Now it was gone. Oliver Cromwell had created nothing that was greater than himself; he was the government and was the only man that could control both the Parliament and the army. Army unity was necessary and there was no unity after Cromwell died. A new strong leader with military experience was required – His successor Richard Cromwell was not that man.

The monarchy was restored in 1660 with more genuine celebration than Charles II could ever have anticipated. It was at this point, with bonfires lit, toasts drunk and effigies destroyed, that Cromwell's reputation reached its nadir. He had been a failure. His regime had survived a mere eighteen months without him. He had created nothing permanent.

Cromwell's post-mortem execution was a deliberate attempt to further ruin his historical reputation. Unlike Cromwell, the executed regicides had the advantage of dying nobly, and they did so mostly in support of their act of regicide, not Cromwell. Some of those hanged, drawn and quartered, like Thomas Harrison, hated him. There was no book of devotional pictures of Cromwell similar to the bestsellers that show pious illustrations of Charles in prayer. The execution of Charles I created a martyr myth that endures today. Cromwell's death did the opposite; it is still seen as gruesome and humiliating.

It seemed all over. The army were paid off, the soldiers went back home, and the causes that Cromwell stood for seemed to be lost. Even people who hated each other hated Cromwell. Republicans hated his aping of monarchy; this united them with the Royalists. Republicans saw Cromwell as a betrayer and a hypocrite; Royalists saw him as an unnatural usurper.

You could make a living in the 1660s by besmirching the name of Cromwell, and hundreds did. The man who earned the most money, but did not live long enough to enjoy it, was James Heath with his book *Flagellum* (1664). Every sin and weakness is here; it is a cut-and-paste compilation of exaggerations, half truths and lies. One of the only strengths is that his bias is so self-evident that the reader is always in a posture of sceptical defence. John Morrill, the great historian of Cromwell's reputation, called Heath 'scurrilous, mendacious, and malicious'.

'Flagellum' may mean 'whip' in Latin, but Heath is not trying to be the author who is lacerating Cromwell. That was far too obvious. The reader already knew Cromwell was evil, and part of his evil was that he was the whip itself, a scourge sent by Satan to punish a wicked nation. Cromwell's rise to power had to be presented as both premeditated and unnatural.

So, among the stories of juvenile naughtiness there is the story of Cromwell as the Apple Dragon, stealing from orchards, and it turns into a religious statement:

> that very offence ripened in him afterwards to the throwing
> down all boundaries of law or conscience, and the stealing
> and tasting the forbidden fruit of sovereignty, by which as
> the serpent told him, he should be like unto a God.

Heath popularised every negative view of Cromwell – ambitious, evil, hypocritical, uncontrollable; deep down no more than a satanic child. *Flagellum* was not only a bestseller, but its lies and distortions were recycled by other authors for centuries afterwards and echoes of Heaths' stories can be heard up to the present day.

The first chink of light for the Protector's reputation came in the late 1660s when it became clear that Cromwell's success abroad was not going to be replicated by Charles II. Cromwell had done well, negotiating on equal terms with foreign monarchs and empires and even capturing Jamaica and Dunkirk. Under his rule, England was (temporarily) a world power, with an army as good as anybody's and a navy that could defeat the Spanish and the Dutch.

That this situation had changed under Charles II was made painfully obvious at the 1665 Battle of Bergen, where the navy was humiliatingly beaten by the Danes and Dutch due to a mixture of poor weather, inefficient diplomacy and a lack of investment. In 1667 the Dutch attacked the fleet anchored at Medway, caused panic in London, and gave the distinct impression that the Stuart monarchy could not even defend England, never mind threaten her enemies abroad.

The diarist Samuel Pepys worked for the Navy Board and knew better than anybody how Stuart underinvestment had adversely affected foreign policy. He recognised Cromwell's success: 'What brave things he did, and made all the neighbour princes fear him.' Pepys reported that other people – not him of course – were commenting that 'it is a miracle that a man [Charles] should devise to lose so much in so short a time'. This part of the quote is less well known; it tends to damn Charles more than praise Cromwell, and it is true to say that the rise in Cromwell's reputation was merely in comparison to Charles's weaknesses.

In 1672, the Dutch ambassador told Charles II to his face that 'Cromwell was a great man, who made himself feared by land and sea'. Charles's reply – 'I will make myself be feared too in my turn', sounded just as lame then as it does today. Even after some compensating military victories it was clear that Charles II was in hock, both financially and politically, to Catholic France. After a string of foreign policy missteps in the 1660s and 1670s, people started to reminisce about Cromwell as a 'hard man' – arguably, in the same way that some people in the turbulent post-Communist Russia of the 1990s longed for the return of a Stalin figure.

This was still a minority opinion. Cromwell remained important in the decades after his death because it suited everybody to emphasise his uniqueness. He was a warning, not just of the dangers of civil war and usurpers, but how an ordinary person could be the agent of chaos. This comment from Robert Smith, a prebend of Westminster Abbey, overstates the Protector's ordinariness to present him as a freak of nature:

> Who that beheld such a beggarly fellow as Cromwell first
> enter the house with a threadbare torn cloak and a greasy hat
> and perhaps neither of them paid for, could have suspected
> that in the course of so few years he should, by the murder of
> one king and the banishment of another, ascend the throne
> and be invested in the royal robes want nothing of the state of
> a king but the changing his hat into a crown. (1685)

Cromwell's reputation was never going to improve for most of the eighteenth century. W.C. Abbott, who collected his speeches, pointed out that Cromwell had managed to alienate both sides of politics in the century after his death. By both executing a monarch and purging parliaments he made enemies of both Tories and Whigs.

It was in the area of religion that he first strengthened his reputation. The 1838 edition of *Primitive Methodist* magazine is an example of the attitudes of hundreds of free churches:

> He had however a main hand in restraining persecution,
> promoting religion and moralizing the English nation to an
> extent never before known ... it rose in morality [and] also in
> dignity showing proof that 'Righteousness exalteth a nation'

From the point of view of Primitive Methodists, the Stuarts were far worse:

> Charles II was a concealed papist and one of the greatest profligates in Europe. His brother … was a more open Roman Catholic. In the accession of Charles II those bishops and others who had shown so much zeal for church ales, revels and Sabbath breaking sports had a king according to their own inclinations.

People who were fighting against unjust monarchs would lean on Cromwell's legacy too. In April 1786, John Adams and Thomas Jefferson, the future second and third presidents of the United States, visited Fort Royal Hill at the Worcester battlefield. Adams gave the locals a lecture on their own history, which he believed they had forgotten. It was about freedom and limited government, which the American rebels thought was the same thing. 'Edgehill and Worcester were curious and interesting to us, as scenes where freemen had fought for their rights', said Adams. Their new republic had just fought a despotic king for their independence and it suited their purposes to interpret the civil war in the same way.

Adams, Jefferson and others like Alexander Hamilton saw much to praise in Cromwell. Like Cromwell, their objection was to unlimited power in one person, not to monarchy itself. Adams, who was in Britain in his role as US ambassador was able to have polite conversations with George III – *after* they had broken his power in the USA. They liked the idea of written constitutions that restricted the power of an individual; so they liked Cromwell. There is an oak tree in the park, planted in 2009 to commemorate their visit.

Chapter Eighteen

Cromwell's Changing Reputation
II – The Age of Statues 1850–1920

Nations don't produce images of people they detest, and by 1901 there were four public statues of Oliver Cromwell in the United Kingdom – that's more than Charles I. Cromwell appears in Warrington, Manchester, St Ives and most famously, outside the Old Palace Yard, near the Houses of Parliament. They all originate from the late Victorian period, when Cromwell's reputation was at its highest outside of Catholic Ireland. The earliest was in Manchester in 1875; the others can be directly linked to the tercentenary of his birth; two of them (Westminster and Warrington) date from 1899, and the later one in St Ives (1901) was a direct result of Huntingdon failing to mark the tercentenary and the people of St Ives stepping in.

The age of statues starts in about 1850, with talking rather than doing, and the process begins with the historian and contrarian Thomas Carlyle. Carlyle resurrected the reputation of Cromwell, providing the antidote to two centuries of gutter journalism by printing his actual words in the form of his collected speeches. This was not an attempt to let people think for themselves. Carlyle provided a tendentious and sometimes splenetic commentary to make the point that Cromwell was a principled and important man. In Carlyle's view, Cromwell was the greatest Englishman who ever lived, especially in comparison to the mediocrities that were being celebrated in his time. Carlyle's favourite example was George Hudson, the 'Railway King', who was exposed as an unprincipled fraud. Carlyle lamented the spirit of the age when crooks were held in high regard. Why not, suggested Carlyle, a statue to Cromwell in Huntingdon? His first attempt was to encourage/browbeat the town council around the 250th anniversary, but this was too soon. Public opinion was not ready. Indeed public opinion was only just coming into existence.

111

None of the statues were built without controversy. It was another generation before anything happened, and then not in any of the obvious places. Seventeenth-century Manchester had been a radical supporter of Parliament and the Victorian city was similar. It was a group of Liberal politicians, led by Thomas Potter, that agitated for a statue of Cromwell, who had never set foot in Manchester at any time in his life. Potter was also a friend of the free trader Richard Cobden and of Giuseppe Garibaldi and presented the city with busts of all three men. It was what Cromwell represented that attracted the Liberals of the city.

The idea was first mooted in 1860 but progress was slow. The original statue was meant to be inside Manchester Town Hall but there was no political will for this, so it was placed on the street outside. Cromwell's reputation among the general population was not as strong beyond some elected politicians, with its Irish residents and its mercantile Conservatives united in loathing him, but many Liberals saw him as an ideal symbol of their progressive city. Thomas Potter, for one, would not dilute his opinions, pointing out that: 'This tardy act of justice to the memory of Cromwell was most appropriate in this great city, where the greatest movements in progress had been carried on.' Wherever Liberals and Nonconformists took power in Britain, Cromwell's stock rose.

The Cromwell statue was moved in the late 1960s, not due to an ideological battle but because he was blocking traffic. Cromwell was moved 5 miles away to Wythenshawe Park, where he remains today. The statue is near Wythenshawe Hall, which is a sixteenth-century timber-framed former manor house. This was the type of house that was besieged in the civil war, as well as the more famous castles and towns, and was taken by Parliament in 1644. It is now a museum with furniture, paintings and weapons from the seventeenth century.

Warrington has a different claim to a Cromwell connection. It declared for the king in 1642, was cleared of its Royalist garrison in June 1643, and remained relatively peaceful until the second civil war. In 1648, when the Royalist army had been defeated at Preston, there was a major mopping-up operation led by Cromwell. He was in town mid-August and bombarded the Royalists in St Elphin's church. The damage to the east chancel wall is still visible today. Warrington was not an instinctively Parliamentary town, like Manchester. To add insult to injury, in August 1651 Warrington was the scene of the last Royalist victory of the civil war when Scots troops under Charles II won the Battle of Warrington Bridge.

Support for a statue came – once again – from Liberal, Nonconformist politicians who believed that Cromwell had done enough for liberty to be called a great Englishman. In this case it was Fred Monks, a relatively lowly born man who became an iron entrepreneur. As a Nonconformist, he would have shared Cromwell's view of Protestantism. The proposed statue was not new in 1899 – it had been shown at an international exhibition in 1862 and had been viewed with disfavour, predictably, by Queen Victoria. In 1899 Monk wrote to the Warrington Council and offered them this statue of a 'remarkable man'. The local council were concerned that it was a political gift and therefore wasn't appropriate. The debate was one that would have been impossible a century earlier, and not just because Warrington would not have had a democratically elected town council. Alderman Henry Roberts (Peoples College, grammar school, self-made brick and tile manufacturer) put forward the idea that he was a great Englishman – despite some of his actions. Dr Cannell believed that he was 'an absolute murderer' and 'a diabolical scoundrel'. Dr Cannell also argued that a man who had cleared, bullied and manipulated parliaments could not be regarded as a friend of democracy.

The vote was won, and the statue erected. The Council had decided that Monk had no political leanings. This was clearly untrue. When Monk died in 1897, the *Warrington Guardian* made this clear:

> In politics he was for many years a convinced and enthusiastic Liberal, but like thousands of other Nonconformists, his anti-Roman proclivities proved stronger than his loyalty to Gladstonian Liberalism.

At the same time, Huntingdon failed to raise enough money and enthusiasm for the tercentenary of Cromwell's birth in 1599 – but they did not try very hard. The Town Council only started to raise funds in January 1899 for a statue that was meant to be unveiled in September of the same year. Only two people contributed a figure of more than £10 and a mere $5 was raised from the United States. St Ives took the initiative, raising the money by public subscription. This was the same method that Huntingdon had used, but sentiment in St Ives was different. The local free churches, stronger in St Ives than they were in Huntingdon, led an effective campaign to raise the money.

The long road to a Westminster statue is a similar story. When the newly rebuilt Parliament was re-opened in the 1840s, it needed new decorative fittings and fixtures. Carlyle, who had just started his Cromwell crusade, predictably called for a statue, or at least a bust. The subject came up regularly, two years in a row in the early 1860s, but given its controversial nature it was an easy decision to postpone.

It was another Liberal who pushed the argument forward. Prime Minister Lord Roseberry was having trouble with what he saw as an over-mighty House of Lords, and Cromwell came to mind. The Liberal cabinet agreed to 'a standing figure of heroic size'. Although it was agreed by the House of Commons, the opposition was so vehement elsewhere that Roseberry decided to become an anonymous donor to finance the statue himself – it cost around £5,000. Once again, the same pattern can be seen – statues appear only when a Liberal, Nonconformist majority can go ahead and ignore the protests of the monarchy, the Conservatives and the Catholic Irish. The fact that the statue was unveiled at 7.30 am on a dull morning in November 1899 showed the need for a low-key event. The problem was the Irish connections; the Liberal government relied on Irish Nationalist votes and they were as reluctant to sanction it as the Irish labourers were to dig the moat to put the statue in.

Part of the reason why the statue went up was that enough Conservatives now regarded Cromwell as a patriot and imperialist, and were able to see past the fact that he was a Radical and Dissenter, which was what the Liberals liked about him. Cromwell suited the Victorian age more than most. He could be lauded as a self-made man, a model of social mobility and a militarist. His position in the twentieth century became more ambiguous.

Chapter Nineteen

Cromwell's Changing Reputation
III – The Age of Ambiguity, 1920–present

Cromwell's favourable reputation persisted into the first few decades of the century. US president Theodore Roosevelt wrote a very partisan biography ('the founder of the freedom of the English speaking peoples') at the turn of the century, consolidating Cromwell's reputation in the English-speaking world. Then the dictators arrived.

In the twentieth century, Lenin was the new Cromwell. For those who liked the comparison, it could be made to work. In both cases, autocracies were overturned by people with extremely strong convictions that changed government and then tried to change people as well. The Communists had the new Soviet Man and the Puritans their reformation of manners. Both had organised their revolt through a small number of people – Cromwell's elect and Lenin's vanguard, and both ended up with a supreme power.

Lenin seemed to give Cromwell's methods, or his interpretation of his methods, some thought. According to a newspaper report of a meeting in the 1920s the Conservative MP Nancy Astor once challenged Lenin on his actions – 'What about your Cromwell?' was his reply.

In December 1933, an 'enemy of Hitler', Mr H. Plunkett Woodgate, told the Edinburgh Philosophical Society that Hitler was the German Cromwell. In 1937, Nazi sympathiser William Harbutt Dawson told an audience at Hull University College that Cromwell was 'Hitler's prototype'. This was common; both sides of the Hitler debate ascribed Hitlerian characteristics to Cromwell; it was a pincer movement that did considerable damage to his reputation

While the enemies and friends of National Socialism compared Cromwell to Hitler, the Nazis themselves had been studying British history and making it work for their own situation. In July 1932, when the Nazis

115

were doing well in Germany but were still fighting free and fair elections, a report in the *Hull Daily Mail* translated one of the Nazi election posters:

> Three hundred years ago, Oliver Cromwell who helped to make England great again, broke up an ineffectual parliament. In Germany it is ALSO time to put an end to their frivolous play!

It has proved difficult to find any provenance for this poster, but it fits with other evidence. Hitler said the same thing in an interview with the New York Times in 1933. We know that Hitler read Cromwell's speeches in translation and admired his determination, his robust treatment of parliaments, and his subjugation of Scotland and Ireland.

The problem with using a historical example as a political slogan is that you know what happened in the end, and Cromwell ultimately failed. As ever, the Nazis could use anti-Semitism as their nasty crutch. They argued that, by tolerating the Jews and allowing them back into the country officially, Cromwell showed that he did not have the courage of a true, iron-willed leader like the Führer.

Mussolini preferred Cromwell to Napoleon. Il Duce liked Cromwell's combination of absolute power and peace at home. He admired his Puritan reformation of manners, which he tried to emulate in Italy. For both Hitler and Mussolini, the Civil War Levellers could be reinterpreted as Communist and Cromwell therefore became a prototype anti-Bolshevik. The Nazis had their own Charles I – the former Emperor William and his family. The Nazis had the same contempt for the Hohenzollerns as Oliver's army had for the Stuarts.

Cromwell's success in foreign policy was compared to Hitler, and those who failed to oppose both men were cast as appeasers. At a Labour meeting in Britain, the French Socialist leader Leon Blum compared the then government of France with the Bourbon kings of the seventeenth century – both appeased dictators and murderers, whether they were Hitler or Cromwell. He then apologised for mentioning Cromwell's name in a left-wing meeting. That was diplomatic. The Labour Party have always been ambivalent about Cromwell.

During the actual war with the dictators, Cromwell's reputation remained precarious. On 19 February 1944, the Westminster statue was nearly destroyed by enemy action. Cromwell's reputation was so well balanced between haters and admirers that it is very difficult to predict whether it would ever have been rebuilt. There were occasional debates in the newspapers. One correspondent to the *Liverpool Echo* wanted the statue melted down for munitions, while others wanted their statue to act as a reminder that general elections, suspended during the war, needed to be remembered. Confusingly, there were Conservatives and Socialists on both sides of the arguments, both using the bits of Cromwell that they liked most.

Some groups supported Cromwell unconditionally. Those who were looking for British heroes who had stood up for freedom concluded that Cromwell fitted the bill. Once again, it was the Liberals who claimed him. In December 1943, the MP Isaac Foot – a man who would tip his hat to the Cromwell statue every time he entered Parliament – noted that the statue of Abraham Lincoln was just in sight of St Margaret's Church where John Pym's bones were interred in 1661. Foot noted that Pym would have been forgotten and Lincoln never come to power without the 'Man Who Saved Parliament'. The liberal historian G.M. Trevelyan interpreted the statue of Cromwell, with Parliament to his rear, as a man of principle defending democracy from arbitrary government; in the Europe of both the seventeenth and nineteenth centuries, it was clear how precarious representative government was. Other newspaper correspondents interpreted his back being turned to Parliament as contempt for the organisation. Then, as now, you could have the Cromwell you desired.

Sometimes ideologies met. In 1919, the future fascist leader Oswald Mosley was campaigning for Nancy Astor – the first elected female MP to take up her seat – when he met a local MP with whom he shared an admiration for Cromwell: Liberal Party MP Isaac Foot again.

After the Second World War, Cromwell was rehabilitated a little. There were still peevish letters to the local papers comparing the Protector's rule with the Hitler state, but as the full inhumane horror of fascism became clearer, the comparison started to look silly. Like Napoleon a century earlier, Cromwell's use of his considerable power was looking more benign. Maurice Ashley, whose biography of Cromwell in 1937 had been called *Oliver Cromwell – The Conservative Dictator* – had changed his mind by 1957, when he wrote *The Greatness of Oliver Cromwell*. He knew more about Cromwell in his reassessment, but, more importantly, he knew considerably more about dictators.

After the war, his reputation was built up by left-wing historians such as Christopher Hill who emphasised his crucial contribution to British political and religious life – a kind of Thomas Carlyle with added Marxism. In the 1970s, the civil war was the 'English Revolution' in the universities, interest in proto-democratic groups increased, and Cromwell became the enemy of democracy because he crushed the Levellers.

In 2002, the BBC conducted a television poll to determine the 100 greatest Britons. Winston Churchill, a man whose many and egregious faults have been forgiven and forgotten by the British and their obsession with the war, topped the poll. It was a poll that was open to manipulation by special interest groups, despite some elementary precautions by the BBC, for example, allowing only one vote from an individual computer or telephone. The *Daily Mail* contended that it was the students of the eponymous university that secured second place for Isambard Kingdom Brunel. This may explain the success of a man who deserves recognition but does not feature much in our school system or national mythology like Dickens, Shakespeare, Elizabeth I and John Lennon, who all made the top ten.

It was not really a poll about historical importance, but a snapshot of people's interests and concerns in the early part of the millennium. The criterion for greatness is not made clear, and the results are therefore a little skewed. Although a much-loved actor, Michael Crawford should not be a mere seven rungs below the Lord Protector. It may have had something to do with his high-profile appearance on the TV chat show *Parkinson* during the polling – this was 2002, before television viewing was atomised by multiple media sources and hard-disk recording. Some others – Diana Spencer (3rd), the occultist Aleister Crowley (76th) and the founder of the internet Sir Tim Berners-Lee (99th) may find their position changed if the poll was done again. It is probably not an accident that the BBC website puts all but the top ten in alphabetical order instead of ranking.

Cromwell finished 10th, sandwiched between Horatio Nelson and Earnest Shackleton, and this feels about right, even if much of the rest is unconvincing. Cromwell's celebratory TV programme was hosted by the military historian Richard Holmes, who admired Cromwell's contribution to parliamentary democracy just as much as his military ability. He also echoed the grudging respect that Cromwell received from the age of Thatcher onwards, when it became possible to admire social mobility without admiring the person or their methods: 'he emerged from obscurity to help give us Parliamentary democracy – our proudest ever achievement. Not bad for a Fenland farmer.'

Cromwell's reputation seems to have taken a turn for the worse at the beginning of the twenty-first century. As ever, it is more to do with the pre-occupations of the present time than any objective view of the past. At present, we worry about religion-inspired armies, terrorism and religious fanaticism. As a man inspired by religion who created an army infused with faith, who later went on to set up a government based on strict moral principles, Cromwell looks to some people like a cross between Osama Bin Laden and the Taliban. In the past, Cromwell has gained credit for raising the reputation of the British armed forces, but it works less well in a world where many armies seem to be religious fanatics. Cromwell's belief that he was an instrument of God does not make him popular today either – the fact that he regarded himself as totally unworthy of God's grace, and dedicated his life to earning His favour, is a part of the complicated story that does not make the headlines.

What do you get when you search #olivercromwell on Twitter, the modern court of public opinion? Cromwell divides opinions a lot because the society that still wishes to talk about him is also divided. In a Twitter search in December 2017, with no major anniversaries to skew the result, the top category was education tweets for books, websites and television programmes. This should be expected for a major historical figure, but it was a mere 15 per cent of tweets. The next largest was opinion – tweets condemning him for his treatment of the Irish (13 per cent). That is probably how it should be – except most people forget that Cromwell was just the figurehead of a system that hated and feared Catholics. It's easier to pick out a scapegoat than analyse a belief system.

The British steam engine named after him comes third, with 11 per cent. It's hard to know whether this says good or bad things about the British people – is it a sign of a forgiving, non-political nature, or just being deluded about their shared past? It is best to remember that the importance of this steam train, and the joy people get from videoing it puffing out of railway stations, will be slightly overestimated in this survey as the train uses this hashtag only, while there are many alternative ones about Cromwell.

The next category – with 10 per cent – includes all the 'Cromwell was here/knocked down this castle /come to our museum', so we could, if we wanted to feel better, add them to the educational tweets, making the total neutral, scholarly tweets about 25 per cent of the total; 8 per cent of cyberspace thought that a supermarket brand of gin was a reason to use #olivercromwell. He would not have agreed!

Seven per cent wished him well, mostly on his birthday, another 6 per cent used his name in a motivational quote and another 5 per cent called him a tyrant, including comparisons with Islamic terrorists. But then 4 per cent hailed him as a lover of freedom and another 4 per cent wanted his statue pulled down. Condemning statues of people with whom you disagree has become a feature of British society and Cromwell is an obvious target.

Seventeen per cent of the tweets were a little unpleasant, and that's worrying. They mostly claimed a link between the tweeter's own views and Cromwell, or glorified war or dictatorships. About ten of the seventeen were objectionable people who thought Cromwell was good. Most were racist. One tweet compared Cromwell to a Muslim fanatic and another said that he would have hated mosques being built in Britain. There is real confusion here!

So the Twitter view of #olivercromwell is 25 per cent neutral, 27 per cent in favour, 29 per cent against and 19 per cent gin and steam engines. What are we to make of that?

Chapter Twenty

Cromwell's Unchanging Reputation
War Criminal and Misery Guts

In England, Cromwell's reputation has fluctuated through time. This is not the case among the Catholic Irish. Cromwell is hated by them for his ruthless treatment of Catholics in Britain and Ireland.

A good example of this kind of treatment can be seen after the Battle of Naseby in 1645, a victory for the Parliamentarian forces. A letter was sent from the commander of the New Model Army to the speaker of the Commons:

> Some Irish are among the prisoners as I am informed I have not time to make enquiry into it. I desire they may be proceeded against according to ordnance of parliament.

The writer was not particularly concerned. As he said himself, there was a parliamentary ordinance covering these circumstances from the year before (24 October 1644). Both Houses of Parliament had agreed that 'no quarter' should be given to any Irishman or any papist born in Ireland. 'When they were taken they should forthwith be put to death'.

The Irish rebels could, and should, be killed. This letter was written not by Cromwell, but by his superior, Thomas Fairfax. Anti-Irish sentiment was part of a bigger worldview shared by thousands of people and many in a position of authority, including what was left of the Parliament in Westminster. It was not just Oliver Cromwell, but as the most successful general, and one who also campaigned in Ireland, he gets most of the blame. It was not just about the Irish as Catholics, it was about the Irish as rebels, as the priests at Basing House were to find out in November 1645. Cromwell's actions were greeted enthusiastically at the time by the vast majority of the English Protestants.

Cromwell is vilified in Catholic Ireland to this day. He tried and executed Charles I as a war criminal, but from an Irish perspective, there is an Englishman whose war crimes were much worse and remain unpunished. The 'Curse of Cromwell' still exists. The *History of Ireland* website recounts this story:

> In 1997, shortly after the Labour Party's victory in the British general election, the newly appointed foreign secretary, Robin Cook, received a courtesy visit from Bertie Ahern. The taoiseach entered Cook's office but immediately walked out again on seeing a painting of Oliver Cromwell in the room. He refused to return until somebody removed the picture of 'that murdering bastard'.

Stephen Fry, who recounted the story, compared the incident to 'hanging a portrait of Eichmann before the visit of the Israeli prime minister'. This is a striking comparison, and underlines the point that it is still acceptable to compare Cromwell with Nazism when the subject is Ireland.

It's hard to understand why there was a portrait of Cromwell in the Foreign Office in the first place, and why nobody thought to move it when the prime minister of Ireland was visiting. It has taken a long time for the British to accept that the Republic of Ireland is a separate sovereign state. Perhaps Cromwell has something to do with that.

Was Cromwell a war criminal? Probably not, in the strictest sense of the word. You cannot be guilty of a crime that did not exist at the time. The rules for war were really only conventions in the seventeenth century and Cromwell obeyed them as much as any other protagonist. Unlike the Red Cross's rules about prisoners, and other laws which established war crimes following the Second World War, there were no international rules that could be enforced by global institutions. In any case, the debate is sterile; Cromwell is often judged by his effect on the Irish, and this needs no label to be resented by many of them.

The most well known modern cultural contribution to this resentment is the song 'Young Ned of the Hill' ('Éamonn an Chnoic' in Gaelic). This is a folk song that recounts the legend of Éamonn Ó Riain (Edmund O'Ryan – that's where the 'Ned' comes from). Ned was a 'raperee', a Robin Hood style figure, who harassed and robbed English troops and landlords and gave money to the Irish Catholic poor.

It comes in different forms – a folk song by the composer Ron Kavana and a punkier version by the Pogues. The main verses are about Éamonn/ Ned, but the chorus is dedicated to a hatred of Oliver Cromwell, and the song remains popular because the sentiment is the same today. Sometimes the song is known as 'God Curse You Oliver Cromwell' and it is a line sung with feeling by the Irish who have not forgotten, nor forgiven him: 'You who raped our Motherland – I hope you're rotting down in hell, – For the horrors that you sent'.

Much of the criticism of Cromwell is fact. Cromwell and his victorious army did push the Irish peasantry into the inaccessible lands of the west, as the song implies, and it seems fact that Cromwell used the expression 'To Hell or Connaught' (Gaelic *Connacht*) to suggest that the rebel Irish could either die in their homes or perish in a part of Ireland not wanted by the new Protestant farmers.

Not all the Irish were pushed out of their lands, but their fate was not much better. Many stayed at home and ended up as workers for new occupiers, including thousands of soldiers of Cromwell's army who settled there. Others were shipped off to be indentured servants – one step up from slaves – in the West Indies. These things are not mentioned in the song, and probably could not make the hatred of Cromwell more intense than the lyrics already suggest.

Cromwell's reputation for denying fun to ordinary people has never left him while other aspects of his reputation have varied over time. This could be because it is true. The first piece of evidence for the prosecution was that Cromwell was a Puritan. Even today, nobody likes being called a Puritan. Nobody wants to be associated with the unsmiling, black and white miseries that abolished Christmas. Cromwell is often blamed for this. He was not personally responsible, but was part of a movement that made it happen – a little like the situation in Ireland.

It was the Puritan movement that started the attack on 'fun'. The assault against Christmas Day started in 1643, just as Cromwell was emerging from obscurity. Puritans had consulted their Bible and found no mention of Christmas. Some MPs, trying to make a point, turned up for work on the day itself. Some Puritan churches failed to open; some shops opened as normal. This was none of Oliver Cromwell's doing, but he approved of it. Around Christmas 1644, the Parliament was still upset about the attitude of the people. 'Christ-tide' (the 'mas' sounded a bit papist) was merely an excuse to 'give liberty to carnal and sensual delights.... In pretending memory of Christ, they had forgotten him'.

Christmas was not included on an approved list of feast days in January 1645 and was officially abolished in June 1647. So the Puritans did deserve the blame for it, and later, when Cromwell was in charge, he actively enforced the law. Throughout the 1650s, people had to celebrate the festival in semi-secrecy. So, the Puritans are guilty of trying to abolish Christmas, and Cromwell has to be guilty, if only by association. The return of authorised Christmas festivities in 1660 was one of the main reasons to be glad that the rule of the Puritans was over.

Cromwell keeps his reputation as a misery guts because, even 350 years later, the British do not want to be reformed and improved. The English were not a very godly nation, despite Cromwell's efforts. They still aren't. They did not want the kind of Sunday that was enforced by both Puritan Parliament and Oliver Cromwell. No sports or pastimes could be practiced during the Sabbath, no work that could be avoided could be done, nothing could be bought or sold; even servants were forbidden to work. People did not want adultery to be a capital offence – when this happened in 1650, juries failed to convict, even in the face of overwhelming evidence.

Anything that could lead to sin was abolished, discouraged, or hunted down. During Cromwell's personal rule as Lord Protector there was an attempt to improve the morals of the country by law and force. From August 1655 until late 1656, England was divided up into regions run mostly by the Puritan major generals, most of whom would have been rudely ignored by the ruling classes before the war; one of them, James Berry, had been a clerk in an iron works. Cromwell introduced them to make the country more godly, among other reasons, and they were overwhelmingly unpopular. Bear-baiting sites were demolished and all of the bears shot; cocks used in fighting were strangled; this was not an issue of animal rights. Horse racing, wrestling, football and dancing were suppressed. The theatre, which emerged around the same time as the Stuart monarchy in England, had already been banned before Cromwell's rule.

The reputation continues – in films like *Cromwell*, in comedy like *Monty Python* and *Horrible Histories*, in the education system and now on social media. In January 2018, early-modern historian Dr Jonathan Healey posted a picture of a chocolate cake on social media with this message:

Oliver Cromwell banned the eating of chocolate cake in 1644, declaring it a pagan form of eating. For sixteen years, cake eating and making went underground until the Restoration leaders lifted the ban on cake in 1660.

This, as *History Today* suggested (March 2018) was 'cake news'. The date – 1644 – was too early, chocolate was not widely available, and the event never happened. However, it was re-tweeted and shared a lot on social media – with only a few people (myself included) being brave enough to doubt it. It fits exactly Cromwell's reputation.

Does it stick because it is true? Was Cromwell a killjoy? From a twenty–first century view, yes, but it depends on what is regarded as important. In the eyes of Puritans, salvation and eternal life were the only prizes a human needed to hope for. What could be more important than being saved from sin? Perhaps we see them as miserable because many of us can only imagine one life on earth. Cromwell was a man of principle – but unfortunately for him, his principles have never really been attractive to the average citizen of this country, so his reputation for being miserable will probably continue.

Chapter Twenty-One

Name in Vain

There is no law preventing people from naming something 'Cromwell', and it has been done to a reasonable extent. If it's called Cromwell Road or Cromwell Tools, it may not be Oliver. London's Cromwell Road is named after the son. There is a Cromwell Road in Stornoway in the Outer Hebrides, but it is named after his soldiers who took the town. Sometimes, Cromwell's name is used deliberately, telling you a lot about the namer and not much about Cromwell.

The record for calling things 'Cromwell' belongs to Winston Churchill. Churchill had some complimentary things to say about Oliver Cromwell. This will probably be regarded as bad news by admirers of either man. There are probably no admirers of both men. Churchill, like many late Victorians, was able to take the bits of Cromwell that he liked and admire those, but still loathe him generally.

Churchill's favourite bit of Cromwell was 'Oliver the war hero', imperialist and all-round British patriot, a view that had been developing since mid-Victorian times. Churchill was First Lord of the Admiralty at a time when the growth of the German navy had become a national concern bordering on panic. However, it was still a surprise to the king when Churchill suggested that one of the new British battleships should be called HMS *Cromwell*. Churchill was attempting to honour the military Cromwell. 'Oliver Cromwell was one of the founders of the Navy and scarcely any man did so much for it. It seems right that we should give to a battleship a name that never failed to make the enemies of England tremble'

Churchill was so keen that he tried twice, and the suggestion was rejected both times by George V. On the first occasion the king felt strongly enough to explain to Churchill in person that he was highly reluctant to name a Royal Navy ship after a regicide. The state of Ireland in 1912, with the Protestant/Unionist north arming and drilling against Home Rule may have been an issue to the king; Churchill, as a historian, would not be able to plead ignorance about the inflammatory effect of the Protector's name on a British warship.

This seemed, and still seems, a reasonable position for the Royal Family to take. Suggestions for names of ships went backward and forward between Churchill for the Navy, and Lord Stamfordham for the king. Other names suggested give an indication of the company that Churchill thought Cromwell was keeping: brave and noble words (Valiant, Liberty, Assiduous, Resolution), success in war (Marlborough, Wellington, Ramillies) and monarchs. Churchill clearly had Cromwell filed under 'successful warriors', but the decision in 1912 that the proposal would be three monarchs and a regicide went down very badly – Lord Stamfordham sending Churchill a testy note reminding him of the king's position.

As a sailor himself, perhaps George was better qualified than Churchill to judge how well these names would be received on the decks. When Churchill suggested the name HMS *Pitt* it was turned down because sailors enjoyed changing the names of ships to something salacious. *Pitt* was too easy.

If Churchill was placing Cromwell in the same bracket as Pitt, it would be important to know which one. It would be fair to say that the Pitt most remembered is Pitt the Younger, who guided Britain through the Napoleonic War with tact, skill, hard work and six bottles of wine a day. This doesn't sound like Cromwell; Churchill had in mind Lord Chatham, the Elder Pitt – Churchill claims in his own *History of the English Speaking Peoples* that this Pitt 'ranks with Marlborough as the greatest Englishman in the century between 1689 and 1786', and that he was the 'first great figure of British imperialism'. This is the Pitt that Cromwell was to be associated with.

Cromwell had been a leader that named ships, though he never named a ship after himself. He removed papist superstition from the names, so the *St George* became the *George*, and he named some after battles like the *Naseby*; one ship was called *Speaker*, an incredibly worthy-but-dull acknowledgement of the importance of Parliament.

There was a HMS *Cromwell* in the Navy very briefly in 1946, but it was transferred to the Norwegian navy under the name *Bergen*. The name

Cromwell appears again, once again courtesy of Winston Churchill, and once again in the context of defence of the realm. In September 1940, Codeword Cromwell was the name given to the warning that a Nazi invasion was imminent; it was actually issued in September 1940 when it was believed that the dictator's forces were on the way.

This seems to be an odd choice, as Churchill later condemned Cromwell as a dictator. In volume two of his hastily written history, he is initially impressed by Cromwell's early success but damns him politically:

> By the end of 1648, all was over; Cromwell was a dictator; the Royalists were crushed; Parliament was a tool; the constitution was a figment.

In this comment, you only need to change the number to something larger to make it sound Hitlerian:

> It was a victory of 20,000 resolute, ruthless, disciplined, military fanatics.

Churchill's Cromwell was an ideologue who gained power by manipulation of other fanatics as a result of a country destroyed by war. Cromwell was Hitler and German militarism. Churchill then went on to reject the view of Liberals who saw Cromwell as a progressive force that sowed the seeds for eventual democracy in Britain. Churchill accused liberals and progressives of picking and choosing which bits of Cromwell they liked, but he did exactly the same.

Churchill's view of Cromwell in Ireland is similar to many people today, but one quote is telling, linking the man's actions to German behaviour in Belgium:

> He therefore resolved on a deed of 'frightfulness', deeply embarrassing to his nineteenth century admirers and apologists.

'Frightfulness' was a word chosen with care. It would have reminded his readers of the alleged murder and massacre of Belgian civilians in the First World War. German militarism condoned violence against the innocent in order to win the war quickly – the same argument as Drogheda, and later, Hiroshima. Churchill extends the German propensity to cruelty to an era before Hitler, and then links the whole era to Cromwell.

How can this man be Churchill's code word for the protection of Britain? Churchill provides a clue when describing Cromwell's rule – Cromwell was a reluctant ruler who used his strength to encourage British commerce and sea power; he scanned the English Channel, both literally and metaphorically, in order to hold back the enemy. Churchill admired this Cromwell and may have seen a parallel with himself – both Cromwell and Churchill were men from a previous time who had found themselves in power after decades of obscurity when Britain was most threatened. In a specific, limited and important way, he was Cromwell himself. Codeword Cromwell makes perfect sense. Churchill saw Cromwell as a laggard from the Elizabethan age, a 'rustic Tudor gentleman, born out of time … in foreign policy he was still fighting the Spanish Armada.'

As mentioned in Chapter 19, when a survey was done of the hashtag #olivercromwell in 2017, the third most popular entry was the eponymous British steam engine. It was one of fifty-five of the 'Britannia' class built for British Railways, completed in 1951 and allocated (by accident, presumably) to run between London and historically Puritan Norwich. It has been a regular guest at stations all over the country, where people make videos of it chugging in and out of stations and excitedly use the hashtag #olivercromwell on social media.

Why was it called Oliver Cromwell and what were the others in the same class called? That would give an indication of the company Cromwell was keeping. They were named after 'Great Britons'. There were other rules; the people had to be dead and their names needed to sound pleasant, and in an interesting reflection on the treatment of the railway employees, the name had to raise rather than depress the morale of the workers. A list of the Great Britons shows a gentle list of largely non-military men. Shakespeare, Chaucer, Burns, and Cromwell's propagandist John Milton are on the list, as is the Puritan John Bunyan. At the beginning of the process there was a bias against military men, so perhaps Cromwell's appearance at the top of the list is a sign that he was there for other reasons. However, another look at the list suggests that military men were acceptable if it was sufficiently long ago (Hotspur, Black Prince, Owen Glyndŵr, Richard the Lionheart). The other famous military strategist on the list was Earl Haig – but this was before 'Oh What a Lovely War!', and 'Blackadder Goes Forth' ruined his reputation.

On the subject of ruin, one successful naming attempt was by the supermarket Aldi, who introduced a Cromwell Dry gin in 2010. It certainly is an anachronism; gin in Britain does not start to infest the back streets of London and poison the lower classes until fifty years after the Lord Protector's death. Cromwell never left Britain and Ireland and would never have experienced the juniper flavoured drink in the Protestant Netherlands where it began. Soldiers who had fought in the Thirty years War may have remembered it – although any who remembered it too well would not be Cromwell's preferred type of soldier.

A gin called Cromwell doesn't really work – historically, anyway. Chris Dugdale in his blog 'Juniper Diaries' has noticed the problem:

> I find it rather amusing that this gin is named after the famous Parliamentarian, Oliver Cromwell (as well as the year of his birth). This famous puritan was rather well-known for being a bit of a kill-joy; while ruling as Lord Protector, Oli managed to close down inns and theatres all over the country, banned make-up, Christmas and most sports.

Most people, I feel would agree. In our modern age, alcohol equates to a good time, and Puritans were the enemies of fun. However, it's a little more complex than that. For a start, it is very doubtful that Cromwell would accept that he was a kill-joy. It is true that he was often moody and melancholic, but he did silly things; he drank alcohol and was known to mess about. I would speculate that if Cromwell was staying overnight in an inn prior to a battle and a gin was available, he would have had one. So many English pubs claim that Cromwell drank in their establishment that it can't just be a marketing ploy.

Why the name? Its full name is '1599 Cromwell Dry London Gin', with the attractive looking date being very prominent on the label. The date, for some reason, gives the bottle some gravitas. As we speak, gin is probably more popular among Britain's fashion leaders than Cromwell himself. There are subtle combinations of common and rare ingredients that make description difficult. And the gin is quite complex too.

There is a hugely successful publishing genre portraying Oliver Cromwell as horrible. This is a trend observable since the civil war was made a compulsory part of the English National Curriculum in 1988.

Despite the schools' best efforts, Cromwell's reputation for the young is at the mercy of the *Horrible History* series of books and television programmes by Terry Deary. Mr Deary is neither a fan of the English school system nor the way that history is taught. Like many well-intentioned people concerned about education, his analysis of schools is based on his era of attendance and not the situation now. History teaching has improved; in the past children were brought up on a solid, indigestible set of dull facts that were neither explained, nor connected to their own life and experiences, and then were asked to memorise them.

This doesn't sound like a recommendation for Deary's work, but the opposite is true. Schools cannot go wrong using his books and television programmes to teach history – his work is always based around fact, and there are few, if any, factually incorrect statements. When it comes to contentious points, the books and TV programmes are even-handed. Cromwell is featured in the *Slimy Stuarts* book, but it is the television programmes that have sealed his reputation, especially the *'Orrible Oliver Cromwell* special.

Each of the main points of Cromwell's character are covered – his seriousness, his obscurity, his lack of concern about his appearance and his rapid rise to power as a military man of action. The programme is also capable of making important points that go beyond the school version of Cromwell. In the sketch *Full Metal Helmet* – the cause of the Parliamentary army's initial success is shown to be Sir Thomas Fairfax, not Cromwell.

The *Cruel Necessity* song provides a simple but not simple-minded explanation of Cromwell's reasons for the execution of the king. The word 'necessity' is explained in a complex way – it was the necessity of 'God's will', not Cromwell merely wishing it to happen. Unlike many funny songs about Cromwell, this one mentions Ireland, but manages to stay funny by not mentioning any details. It has nothing to say about Drogheda and Wexford. The song mentions the Nominated Parliament, which replaced the Rump in 1653 when Cromwell and the army purged it ('Cruel necessity' again). The song accurately shows the problems that Cromwell had with his later parliaments – they were indeed whingers, about money, religion and power – exactly the problems that the execution was meant to solve.

Horrible Histories is useful, despite being simple. The fact that many in Britain would have been taught a simple version of his life makes him no different to Winston Churchill or Queen Victoria. There are no factual errors in the programme. If each British citizen watched and remembered the content of it, then the educational authorities would certainly be satisfied.

Another Cromwell book aimed at young people is Alan MacDonald's *Cromwell and His Not-So Civil War*; when first released in 2000 it had the much more ingenious title of *Oliver Cromwell and his Warts*. Cromwell is on the cover of my edition with his two warts and his stern expression. The book is designed to entertain children, so it needs to be interesting; there is also an unspoken desire to educate, so it uses funny examples but does not mislead. When something about Cromwell is an opinion, or comes from a dubious source, this is acknowledged.

The technique is clear – lure in the reader with a light-hearted tone and lots of jokey facts, especially at the beginning when the book claims that in 1953 five gallons of 'smelly creosote' – most adults would not need the adjective – was thrown over Cromwell's statue outside Parliament. It brilliantly reminds people that the issue has not gone away, although in this unusual case the fact is not quite right. It was the St Ives statue that was covered in creosote.

Sometimes the book's jokes are so good that they can be a useful analytical tool for the Cromwell story. Little is known about Cromwell's time as an MP in the 1620s. We know that Cromwell found it tiresome and his performance was undistinguished. He was not even the most well-known member of his own extended family. MacDonald calls it 'The House of Cousins'.

> He already had nine cousins sitting in parliament so it was a
> bit like being invited to a big family occasion (lots of speeches
> and very little fun).

This is exactly how it was, and explains so much of their behaviour both in the 1620s and during the civil war. It's a concept that professional historians would need to consider; and it is also a joke. That is a difficult thing to pull off.

There are other memorable lines. The Rump Parliament is described as 'a bum deal all round', and some of the lines could be the start of an essay: 'If Oliver had a master plan to become King Oliver I, he was pretty good at hiding it'.

The jokes support the narrative; the only way that it moves from accuracy is by giving undue importance to the grisly and unusual, but in each case it is a hook for something educational. As the civil war progresses through the pages, the jocular language remains the same but the accuracy is maintained. You are reading a history book. Just don't tell the children.

Chapter Twenty-Two

Cromwell on Film

Cromwell (1970)

The most famous film depiction of Cromwell comes from the 1970 film of the same name; and there lies the problem. The interpretation is warped by the need for drama, the natural desire to put Cromwell in the centre of the action at all times, and the need to present a simple version of his character that works on screen.

The film opens with Cromwell looking moodily at some flooded lands that are standing in for the Fens. The fact that they are not drained should have pleased him. Yet he is grumpy; in fact he is grumpy throughout the film, whether he is getting his own way or not. He wants to emigrate, due to the terrible way that England is governed and the inability of the godly to worship freely. This is accurate – he threatened to leave the country in November 1641 if the king's power was not reduced – but he wasn't in the middle of packing in November 1640, as the film suggests.

The film cuts to his so-called home, a palace – in Cambridge – a place he did not live in 1640, or indeed ever. He is visited by two 'friends' that in reality he hardly knew at that point in the story: John Pym and Henry Ireton. He seems to have no knowledge of the Scottish wars when told about them by John Pym, who correctly predicted a new Parliament would be called and it would be a chance to wrest back some power from the king. Cromwell then declares loyalty to the king and a concern at the prospect of civil war, accurately showing his view, and that of almost everybody in the country in 1640.

The main, recurring mistake is that Cromwell is presented throughout the film as the 'Champion of Democracy for the Common People'. This probably suited the makers of the film, and it is still popular today among Cromwell's supporters, but has no basis in fact at all.

Cromwell is seen in the film defending the rights of the poor, which is not the same thing as granting them political power – in this case, it was the traditional right to use common land. This land was used for food, fuel and feeding their animals, in other words: their survival. The film needs Cromwell to be a social progressive, but in reality Cromwell was a traditionalist when he supported the long-established rights of the poor. The drainers and improvers were the, not people like Cromwell.

Cromwell did speak up against the draining of the Fens both in and out of Parliament. The film shows Cromwell squaring up to the Earl of Manchester as the common people try to defend their right to pasture very modern-looking cows (why not sheep? they would have been cheaper, more accurate and less bother). Unlike the scene shown in the film, Cromwell did not use violence. He did clash with the Earl of Manchester politically, and this helps to explain Oliver's mixed feelings about him when they were on the same side during the early civil war.

The 'puritan' part of his character is done quite well, but is not very deep. Hollywood does not make money from an anxious Christian worried about the authority of bishops or whether altars should be railed in, but we do see Cromwell smashing up the altar of the parish church because it has a crucifix on it. This is an undocumented event, almost certainly fiction, but considering the iconoclasm that Cromwell organised later, we can probably let it pass.

Cromwell rose from obscurity in 1640 to being a well known Member of Parliament by January 1642, but the film takes the liberty of making him one of the five MPs that the king decided to arrest, and to make the error worse, he is shown refusing to run away and calling the king's bluff. People like Cromwell were only six months away from doing this in real life; but the film distorts the chronology to make the best of a famous historical event. Fair enough.

Cromwell is featured at the Battle of Edgehill, where the film does a good job explaining the logistics of warfare and, within the limitations set by a feature film, shows the desperate fighting. Cromwell is brave and reckless, starting before the agreed time and standing his ground when Manchester orders a retreat.

The main problem is that Cromwell was not present at the beginning of this particular battle. The reason for this fiction is sincere. It shows that Cromwell was much more fanatical about defeating the king than the Earls of Manchester and Essex. It is clear that Cromwell and people like him understood the logic of fighting the war to the bitter end, rather than just the half-hearted attempt of the two fat, chicken-leg scoffing aristocrats straight from central casting.

The formation of the New Model Army is difficult for a film; it is portrayed as an army that simply learnt to fight properly, not the religious army that it was. There is a good attempt when, in prayers before battle, the Parliamentary hellfire preacher Hugh Peters is shown in black, and the Royalist preacher in scarlet, and Cromwell says that he wishes to create an army 'with fire in their bowels, who fear the Lord and not the enemy'. You would not know from the film that the civil war was mostly short and brutal skirmishes. Cromwell's brilliance as a strategist is reaffirmed by the fiction that Cromwell was outnumbered at Marston Moor and Naseby, but the film also makes clear that the discipline of the Parliamentarian cavalry was a reason for the king's defeat.

In the film there is no second civil war, no 'pass the parcel with the king's person' between the Scots, the army and Parliament. There is no mention of Presbyterianism or the development of a new constitution, both of which would be fatal for ratings and box office takings. The power of the army is acknowledged as Cromwell negotiates for them. Cromwell accidently has some rebellious soldiers executed and regrets it afterwards – this was a fictional account of the 1647 Ware mutiny. The film shows the duplicitous side of the king and the manner in which Cromwell decided that a trial was the only answer. It fails to reference the fact that Cromwell and others saw a message from the Almighty in Charles's defeats – once again, executions inspired by God were not a good look for a film; and that hasn't changed.

The trial in Westminster Hall is done well. The king has his accusers in constitutional knots while Cromwell growls and fulminates. In reality, the king was enclosed in a wooden dock on four sides, but in the film, sight lines demand that he sits alone in the middle of the hall with two guards. In reality, the army was much too scared that somebody would organise an escape. Cromwell is then accurately shown cajoling the other judges to sign his death warrant.

After the execution at the Banqueting House (portrayed very accurately – many of the king's actual words are used) the film goes horribly wrong. In a complete reversal of the truth, instead of the appalling fighting in Ireland (touchy) and Scotland, he goes home and sits by the fire with his pet – a big, un-Puritan looking dog.

Six years later in 1655, some Puritans, many already dead in real life, visit him and call on him to be king. Britain had become ungovernable – this was true. Cromwell laughs in their faces at the offer of kingship – far from true. Then, after saying he will do nothing to help, the next scene shows him going back in time to 1653 and removing the corrupt and rotten Parliament and taking power himself. His enemies would say that was accurate; but then the film finishes with Cromwell promising to build a godly nation, stuffed with schools and hospitals, having remembered that he was a democrat. That is not what happened at all.

Cromwell is a great film, based on history, but it is not a film about history. The bits that matter are mostly accurate, and you can have a great time spoiling it for others after reading about the subject. Do not forget to point out that the old, grimy, falling-down gravestones you see in various shots should be brand new like they were at the time, and that Cromwell's son Oliver did not die bravely in battle, but died from smallpox (or perhaps typhoid) in Newport Pagnell; which is still a tragedy, but not one that works too well on film.

To Kill a King (2003)

The most recent film that claims to be about Oliver Cromwell completely changes the view of him. Instead of the 1970 brooding, moody man of principle we have the near psychopath with an almost unhealthy relationship with Thomas Fairfax. This does not make it a bad film, but makes an unreliable one in its depiction of Cromwell – and everybody else for that matter.

Nothing is covered before Naseby in 1645, and the film starts after the battle for two reasons. One is that this is a relatively low budget film, and wars on film, like wars in real life, are expensive. It accurately portrays Fairfax and not Cromwell as the driving force of the New Model Army, and Cromwell never wastes an opportunity to give Fairfax all the credit. This is because *To Kill a King* is essentially a buddy bromance with two seventeenth-century officers rather than New York Cops, and Cromwell loves Fairfax as a brother and Fairfax feels nearly as strongly, but not quite. Cromwell is the earnest, bad cop with a relatively insecure background and Fairfax is the dashing, handsome one from a rich background. Some of this is true; Cromwell was minor gentry and Fairfax was from a rich

Yorkshire family, but this truth is used to create a myth that an intense relationship existed between the two men.

Anne Fairfax is a key part of the film, as the kind of strong woman that did exist during the civil war, and has (rightly) become a compulsory part of modern films depicting the past. In order to make a sharp contrast, Elizabeth Cromwell, Oliver's wife, is wrongly presented as a bullied frump who could not make pottage without her guests puking up. Although inaccurate, it did reflect the lies that were told about her at the time; perhaps the filmmakers were still reading the same biased Royalist sources.

There is plenty of verisimilitude in the film until the last twenty minutes, where, like *Cromwell*, it goes off the rails when the exciting stuff is over. The Parliament is shown plotting to betray the army. The film accurately shows the diverging opinions of the two men, with Cromwell coming gradually to the conclusion that the king could not be trusted. Rupert Everett is an excellent, mean-looking king who rips enough treaties to make the point, but the army is not really mentioned at all. There is no room in the film for the second civil war either, and it seems hard to understand why Cromwell came to the conclusion that the king had to die. This Cromwell is not very military, only a little religious and occasionally political. He is mostly angry, fed up and jealous.

The two main characters wrangle and fight through most of the film, to the point where it becomes hard to work out why they were friends in the first place. The bromance has a strong hint of the homoerotic about it; Cromwell is clearly jealous when Thomas is with his lovely wife Anne, but it is not always completely clear who he was actually jealous of. The low point (of an entertaining film) is when Fairfax accuses Cromwell of continuing his persecution of the king out of spite because Cromwell is jealous of his attractive wife.

The major objection to the film is that Cromwell is presented as a psychotic monster, ready to do anything to protect his friend Fairfax and defeat his enemy Charles Stuart. Cromwell beats people to death, tortures them using a form of waterboarding, kills spies and dips his hands in the severed head of Charles I. There are other examples and all are completely unhistorical. The Banqueting House is portrayed accurately, although pedants would say that Charles comes out of a window at the wrong side, and the size of crowd was more indicative of a film running out of money than the only public execution of a monarch in England.

You do not have to be a pedant to object to Cromwell being on the scaffold with Charles and smearing himself with the dead king's blood, while lecturing the crowd on the fact that they were now free. The film makes the same mistake as most films: that Cromwell believes in democracy – that is when he is not killing people.

Ironically, the part of history where Cromwell had a reputation for bloodthirstiness – Drogheda and Wexford – is not mentioned at all in the film. Neither is Scotland. It would take away from the tabloid newspaper style rows about relationships.

Cromwell becomes Lord Protector almost immediately. Hampton Court, one of his palaces in real life, is used as a regular location, although the rows of executed traitors are imaginary.

It is rumoured that at the last minute the film title was to be changed to 'Cromwell and Fairfax'. That would have been a good idea, because that is what it is really about.

Chapter Twenty-Three

The State of the Head of the Head of State
Travelling Skull 1661–1960

It took an unusually large number of strokes of the axe to separate the skull from the body. It was done in anger, and not very professionally. Some of the cuts were at the base of the skull rather than the neck, and the nose seems to have been disfigured. As the executioner attempted the decapitation, the nose would have been pressed against a hard surface and would, in its putrid state, be squelched into a gooey mass.

Was this particular skull that of Oliver Cromwell? Yes, it almost certainly was.

The remaining parts of Cromwell have not been found. Their exact location is unclear; that was the intention. Wherever his body was buried, the revengeful Royalists would have made special efforts to ensure that it was in un-consecrated ground. This post-mortem execution took place on 30 January 1661 – exactly twelve years after the execution of the king. Bradshaw and Ireton were the other victims. All heads were put on the top of Westminster Hall, where they had tried their king, usurped his power and set up a sham government, as poetic justice and a reminder of the punishment for treason. In 1685, there was a storm in London and the head started on its travels.

The two other heads are lost to history at this point, but after the storm Cromwell's head was found by a sentry who knew it was important but did not know what it was – or so he claimed later on, somewhat unconvincingly. It is just possible a young, lower-class guard might have had a failing remembrance of how important Cromwell was; a generation had passed. However, those in charge had not forgotten and there was a hue and cry (and a royal proclamation) to locate the head. So, it seems plausible that the myth that it was hidden in a chimney flue is correct; the guard would be too scared to take it out, or give it back.

The head may have resurfaced in the 1710s in the London 'cabinet of curiosities' of an eccentric called Claudius Du Poy. This suggests that Cromwell was, quite literally, a museum exhibit of no importance. Cromwell's head was exhibited alongside roomfuls of unconnected oddities including a pagan idol – 'a large wooden one with an asses head', urns, magnets, and a snake skin 16ft long. Clearly the head had lost some of its political power, partly due to the passage of time and partly to the diminishing proof of providence as 'the' skull.

There is a disturbing gap between the 1710s and 1773, when a skull with the same story attached was in the hands of a Samuel Russell who put it on display, after failing to sell it to Sidney Sussex College. It was available for the public to examine in Clare Market, London, in the 1780s, which was probably an attempt to exploit the interest in republicanism caused by the French and American revolutions. Samuel Russell was not always sober when he hawked the head around London and seemed happy to let people play with it unsupervised – this could explain why part of the ear is missing and his hair and beard short, despite both being allowed to grow in the last few weeks of his life in 1658.

It was owned by a James Cox from 1787 to 1799 when it was purchased by the Hughes brothers, who exhibited it for a short time in their French Revolution exhibition. It may well have been that the Hughes brothers were, in the words of one mid-Victorian magazine, 'violent democrats'. The interest in Cromwell as a political icon was limited, possibly further dampened by the 2s 6d admission fee. (A weaver's wage was about 12s a week and a servant £3 a year)

This advertisement appeared in the *Morning Chronicle* in March 1799:

> The Real Embalmed Head of the Powerful and Renowned
> Oliver Cromwell styled Protector … at No 5 in Mead Court
> Old Bond Street where the rattlesnake was shown last year.

The fact that you were meant to have your memory jogged by remembering last year's celebrity snake, suggests that the show was for an audience of curiosity seekers rather than ardent republicans.

From 1814, the head was in the charge of members of the Wilkinson family; first Josiah, from Sandgate, near Folkestone in Kent and then passed through the family. It is the Wilkinsons who provided the provenance for the head at this point. One of their pieces of paperwork, according to Wilkinson in the Victorian newspapers, was a deed of sale between Russell and Cox.

It is the 'Wilkinson head' that is buried in Sydney Sussex College and the head's progress between 1814 and 1960 is secure. It is actually very secure, because constant generations of the family refused to let it out of their sight. When Josiah Wilkinson acquired the head, it was suggested that he followed current, more sensitive attitudes to these matters and bury it. 'Why would I bury it? My family would not like it!' he was alleged to have said. In any case, his successors were true to their word, holding on to it until 1957.

The head moved upmarket; now it was examined by Wilkinson's academic and establishment friends. It was only on display to invited guests of Wilkinson's family, and removed from its oak box only on special occasions; it was held by the wooden spike rather than played about with. Part of Wilkinson's crusade in favour of the head was his willingness to show anybody who was interested, even if they did not have the technical knowledge to authenticate it. In 1855 Wilkinson was addressing the Walworth Working Men's Institute, boasting that he had the head and invited any interested parties to view it.

Wilkinson's visitors may have been browbeaten into believing. Of the hundreds who had seen it, only one, who had a lock of Cromwell's hair before his death, denied the authenticity of the head. That person was persuaded that the lock of hair they owned had probably turned grey over the passage of time. Cromwell was ginger, but only when alive.

The authenticity of the Wilkinson head came under some doubt in the Victorian era. Thomas Carlyle, not a man for relics at the best of times, characteristically declared it 'fraudulent moonshine', but, equally characteristically, failed to even look at it.

In the February 1864 edition of *Notes and Queries*, Horace Wilkinson described the skull:

> The skin covering the skull is hard but in excellent preservation. The hair moustache still remains and the wart also which is represented in his portraits is plainly to be seen [his] flesh has been embalmed which would not have been the case with the remains of an ordinary person.

When else in history had a preserved head been cut off after death and rammed on to a stick? This was the strength of the Wilkinson argument. It was also the weakness, because every potential forger knew that had happened as well.

Other arguments also could backfire. If Wilkinson was correct that it had appeared in the exhibitions of Russell, Cox and Hughes, that could merely prove it was a showman's fake. The fact that the American and French revolutions increased interest in Cromwell was also more of a motivation to forgery. And there were other heads around.

The Wilkinson family had collected historical approvals from various people who had examined the head and made successful comparisons with portraits and medals. One was from as early as 1775, by a John Kirk of Bedford Street, Covent Garden, who noticed similarities in the nostrils and cheek bones.

The main rival skull was in the Ashmolean Museum, Oxford, and had been on display since 1834 or before. One literary magazine was a little scathing, calling it 'one of the skulls of Oliver Cromwell'. Other myths that muddied the water were that Cromwell's body was switched before the execution, or that it was buried at the Naseby battlefield. The last was an invention of a Victorian curate who perhaps didn't consider why Cromwell would be buried in un-consecrated ground.

In 1844 the provenance of the head received a boost when Wilkinson granted an interview to a journalist, Mr Donovan. Donovan provided a sketch of the head bearing a very strong resemblance to the Hughes brothers' poster of 1799. Donovan was also told that the Hughes brothers were republicans, which may explain why their illustration has the laurel leaves of military victory around his head. With the wreath, the shape of the pole and the direction that it is pushed into the skull, it is clearly the same head. This links the Wilkinson head with the earlier one, confirming that Wilkinson did buy this particular item and extends the provenance of the head to 1773 – assuming of course that Donovan had not seen the 1799 poster. Donovan added his own supporting evidence. There was a hole on the face where the wart would have been – 'the excrescence having fallen off'. The spike through the skull had clearly been with it for a long time.

Donovan was, unfortunately, working for the *Phrenological Journal* and went on to the measure the skull, and, perhaps not surprisingly, discovered personality traits that Cromwell was known to have possessed. This did not help the head's credibility very much when it was re-examined after 1844, as phrenology was regarded with suspicion by an increasing number of scientists; a phrenological endorsement was counter-productive.

This was one of the main arguments of William Pinkerton, who returned to the story in the 1864 edition of *Notes and Queries*. His argument was threefold: anything concluded by a phrenologist must be suspect, by definition; the argument that an embalmed head helps the provenance was untrue, because the evidence that it was embalmed at all was scanty; and the documents held by the Wilkinson family were no more than a showman's patter. However, he seems to have been alone in his belief that the body was not embalmed. Most other commentators, hostile and sympathetic, seem to agree that it was.

Pinkerton provided only negative evidence that the head was not embalmed – the fact that George Bate, Cromwell's doctor, did not say that it was. Bate did provide some other information: 'that the intestines were removed and their place being filled with spices ... the body was wrapped in a six fold cerecloth put into a leaden coffin and the last into a strong wooden one. Yet the corruption burst through.'

Cerecloth was fabric impregnated with wax to form an airtight body-shaped layer. It was part of a high status burial, as was embalming. As Bate suggested, the embalming did not work well, and on the day of Cromwell's funeral, he had already been interred for weeks, and his funeral hearse was empty.

Not everybody accepted Pinkerton's conclusions, and ironically, their arguments were based on the shape of heads, if not the pseudo-scientific conclusions drawn from it. Medallists, sculptors and artists who had been given a personal audience with the head all replied to say that the shape, size and features were the same as Cromwell's.

In 1875 the Wilkinson and Ashmolean exhibits went head to head, so to speak. Sir William Rolleston declared that the Wilkinson head was much more likely to be genuine than the Ashmolean one; the Oxford exhibit did not even seem to be embalmed. Embalming was the key; no forger would have gone to that amount of trouble. The Ashmolean Head was also rather small – some Victorian jokers suggested that it was the skull of Cromwell as a boy.

The first clear breakthrough for the skull came in 1911, when it was exhibited at the Royal Archaeological Society. The majority of scientists declared it genuine. There were too many similarities in too many areas, and too many technical aspects that were outside the scope and interest of the forger. One sign of its new status was the increasing demand in the newspaper columns for the head to be buried somewhere more appropriate – his original resting place in Westminster Abbey was often suggested. After all, Charles I was laid in consecrated ground in Windsor when Cromwell was in charge of *his* earthly remains, so how about justice for Cromwell, said the Liberal press and the Nonconformist churches.

His stock had risen so much by the beginning of the nineteenth century that there were calls in Parliament for the government to purchase the remains and rebury them. Mr Asquith, the Liberal prime minister, declined to do so in 1911, hiding under the argument that their provenance was too precarious. He may not have known that in 1910, the Minster of Works had written to the Wilkinson family on the recent death of Horace Wilkinson in 1908 and requested the skull. They refused; the item was passed on to the last Wilkinson owner, Horace Ricardo Wilkinson.

The Wilkinson crusade for the skull was mostly complete by the 1930s, when cranial experts Pearson and Morant concluded that it was genuine. They pointed out that the skull had been cut open to empty the brain of its contents and this very rare process was only done as part of the embalming of a royal figure. In the 1950s there was an exhibition of Cromwelliana at Hinchingbrooke House, which, although not including the head, was the point at which the Cromwell Association accepted that the head was probably genuine.

Canon Horace Wilkinson died in 1957, leaving the impressive sum of £29,000 and a box with the Protector's head, which was stored at the bottom of his bed. Once again, the family continued the tradition of passing the relic to the eldest son, but he wanted it buried. This happened in March 1960 in a secret ceremony that was not revealed until more than two years later. The oak box was placed in an airtight container.

Nobody really doubts the genuine nature of the head now, even though rival skulls appear occasionally, such as the 1979 Grantham skull, which did not even have a spike. The head is securely buried and there will be no DNA testing. In any case, the last direct Cromwell relative died in 1821. There may not be any direct ancestors left, but when it comes to discussions of religion and politics, we are still the children of Oliver Cromwell.

Further Reading

I have not included any detailed information about the places mentioned as this will change over time. Current details are available online. There are many other places associated with Cromwell, although the major ones are covered in the book. The best online resource for all things Oliver Cromwell is *olivercromwell.org* and its creator, the Cromwell Association. Anything by my former tutor John Morrill will be fascinating.

This book would have been impossible to write without Peter Gaunt's *Cromwellian Gazetteer*, which lists all the places he visited, including slightly less well known places that readers might be interested in. It is an invaluable work of reference.

There are many hundreds of biographies of Oliver Cromwell. Those who become utterly fascinated by every detail should read Antonia Fraser's *Our Chief of Men*. The classic biography, one that emphases his Puritanism, is *Oliver Cromwell And The Rule Of The Puritans In England* by Charles Firth – a free ebook. For a more concise work, try the Cromwell book in the *History in an Hour* series. For Cromwell as Lord Protector, read *In a Free Republic* by Alison Plowden. If you want to be clear about the difference between the two famous Cromwells, the best general introduction to Thomas Cromwell is Kevin Hughes *Thomas Cromwell – Master and Servant*.

The best overview of the era is John Schofield's *From Cromwell to Cromwell* which does what it says on the tin. A very good social history of the civil war is Diane Purkiss's – *The English Civil War*, which covers some fascinating topics that are not part of this book. For the general effects of warfare, try John Barratt's *Sieges of the English Civil War* and *Going to the Wars* by Charles Carlton. Two other books that put Cromwell in the context of the time are the nicely illustrated Channel 4 book *Civil War* by Taylor Downing and Maggie Millman and Tristram Hunt's *English Civil War at First Hand*. For an advanced read, try *Britain in Revolution* by Austen Woolrych.

Bodies and embalmed heads are covered by two books – *The Corpse as Text: Disinterment and Antiquarian Enquiry* By Thea Tomaini and Bess Lovejoy's *Rest in Pieces: The Curious Fates of Famous Corpses*. If you are interested in the Levellers – try Peta Steel's pamphlet issued by the South East regional TUC or, for a longer read, *The Levellers* by John Lees is painstakingly researched for detail. A wider context is available in *A Radical History of England* by Edward Vallance.

The speeches of Oliver Cromwell and the centuries of hostile and friendly biographies, such as those by Heath, Noble, and Carlyle, are available online for free, as are his selected speeches. Type the Lord Protector's name in an internet book search, newspaper search, or social media and then observe the deluge of opinions.

Index

148